birth in the eden environment

no fear involved

Jackie Wiebe

ISBN: 978-0-9977171-2-9

Photo 23188455 © Xunbin Pan | Dreamstime.com

Printed in the United States of America

This book is intended to provide helpful and informative material on the subjects addressed. Nothing in this book is intended as professional medical, physical/mental health, or fitness advice. Please consult with your personal healthcare provider regarding any suggestions or recommendations made in this book. The author expressly disclaims responsibility for any adverse affects arising from the inferences drawn, use, or application of the information in this book.

Thank you to every mother and family who has trusted and
honored me to hold a place in their birth space.
Thank you to the women who allowed me to share their stories, and
to those who helped me review and critique this book.

I love you all!

contents

introduction   7

1 restored to original   11

2 no fear involved   25

3 what about the pain?   45

4 satisfaction vs. disappointment   59

5 physiology of sex & birth   75

6 the need for intimacy   87

7 choice   95

8 choosing a birth team   109

9 natural things matter too   129

10 learn the basics   147

11 have a vision & be led   167

12 healing a broken heart   185

closing   199

introduction

It was November 29th, 2012, and I was pregnant with baby number six after standing in faith for about a year to conceive and carry to full term. During that time two of our little ones went on to Heaven ahead of us. When things like that happen that are not the perfect will of God, people often respond in one of two ways. Either they believe lies about why it happened in order to try and make sense of it, or they are more determined than ever to seek the truth about God's will, character, and intentions in the situation, even if it means taking more time to get real, honest answers. For me it was the latter. I always said I'd rather not know why then to believe lies about why, especially lies about God's character and nature. More than ever before, I wanted to know how God sees pregnancy and birth, and how He originally intended and designed it to be. And so, on this particular day, I asked Him:

"What was birth like before sin?"

The immediate response kind of surprised me.

"There was no fear involved."

That wasn't exactly the answer I expected, maybe because I was thinking more in natural terms, you know…"But what was it *really* like?" However, the more I thought about it the more I realized that really is the ultimate answer to every question or issue surrounding pregnancy and birth in every realm. It's the answer in the natural body, backed by science. It's the answer in the soul, for a sound mind and healthy emotions. And above all, it's the answer in the spirit, because fear tolerated is faith contaminated.

While the primary reason I initially stepped into birth work was to offer help to mothers of babies who were not conceived the way God intended, I've repeatedly seen how vital this message of God's original intent in birth is, not only for these types of mothers, but for all moms, dads, and families. Even in the church, among believers, there has been enormous fear, misinformation, and ignorance in this area, and yet, it's one of the most weighty things we'll ever do or experience. As such, we really need God's perspective on it.

So, when I began to sense the Lord's leading to write this book, I got excited! It's a product of years of journaling, asking questions, observing, and learning. Any revelation I share I had to first receive myself. I had to be taught, and boy, have I learned a thing or two! My mindset on birth has been completely transformed since I first started having babies. I thank God for His faithfulness to lead and guide us step by step, never just leaving us where we are, but always drawing us and taking us higher.

I pray that as you read this book the eyes of your heart be flooded with revelation and insight, that there be many lightbulb moments, that you receive healing, and that you see the beauty, safety, and pure joy in what you were perfectly designed by God to be able to do: bring forth new life!

1 restored to original

My initial quest to seek the Lord about what pregnancy and birth were like before sin, and how to have that kind of birth experience today, has continued throughout the years. Obviously, it didn't happen by chance or just divinely fall on you by sole merit of being a believer, as I'd personally seen and heard of many scenarios, among believers and unbelievers, that were definitely not Eden-like. While the absence of fear, as God said, is the master key, I've learned there are many elements that play into creating and cultivating that type of environment.

Everything God created and designed is good (Genesis 1:31), and has an original intent. One of my increasingly favorite definitions of the word faithful is "true to the original". In order to be true, or faithful, to the original design and purpose of God for us in birth, we need a deep understanding of what that was and always has been. We have to go back to the beginning to get an accurate, clear picture of what a fear free, Eden birth environment looks like.

The conditions and atmosphere of Eden were God's original and unchanging intent for humanity. This was a place and time where things were as He actually *wanted* them to be for people. Eden was saturated with the presence of Love Himself. There was no fear because there was no sin, nor curse, nor any hurtful consequences brought on by sin. Perfect love left no room for fear. There was no sorrow because there was no separation between God and mankind. It was an atmosphere of perfect peace, meaning nothing was missing and nothing was broken or nonworking. It was also an atmosphere full of joy, not just seriousness and somberness, because in the presence of God there is fullness of joy! (Psalm 16:11)

The very word Eden means "pleasure, luxury, and delight". We usually think of it as the place of man's pleasure, and rightly so, because the presence of God produces pleasure. "At Your right hand are pleasures forevermore." (Psalm 16:11 NKJV) However, just as much so, it was also a place of God's pleasure. According to Genesis 1:31 (NASB), His creation gave Him pleasure. "God saw all that He had made, and behold it was very good." Eden was a place where humanity had unbroken fellowship and relationship with God, meaning they fully trusted and believed Him. Clearly that also gave Him untold pleasure, because according to Hebrews 11:6, our faith is what pleases Him! What's more, in Eden, mankind prospered in every way and area - spirit, soul, and body - which is the complete embodiment of the word prosperity. Psalm 35:27b (NKJV) says, "Let the Lord be magnified, Who has pleasure in the prosperity of His servant." He absolutely loved to see His children living in His perfect, original plan for them. Eden was pure pleasure for both God and man!

In this luxurious and delightful place, only meeting basic needs like nourishment, water, shelter, and clothing (they were clothed with God's glory), was not good enough for God. He also wanted to give them pleasure through beauty. Genesis 2:9 (NASB), "Out of the ground God caused to grow every tree that is pleasing to the sight *and* good for food." (emphasis mine) God created beauty for us to enjoy! Beauty matters to Him because He knows how it ministers to us. It's also a glimpse of Heaven on earth. II Chronicles 3:6 and Exodus 28:2 speak of how the house of God was decorated for beauty, and the clothing of the priests was designed for beauty. That which ministers to you through your senses is also an important part of the Eden atmosphere. It wasn't ugly, cold, sterile, and uncomfortable. Interestingly, I've heard people say they chose a birthing location based only on pictures they saw. Because it was so beautiful and inviting, they thought, "*That* is the kind of place I want to have my baby!"

It's also interesting to note the names of the four rivers that split off of the river flowing through Eden. Pishon means "increase", Gihon means "bursting forth", Tigris means "rapid", and Euphrates means "fruitfulness". Those words describe the overflow of a place of intimacy with God - the Eden environment.

Eden was also a place of work. Yes, you read that right! Work, in and of itself, was never a result of the curse brought on by sin. The curse is simply what put heaviness, difficulty, pain, fatigue, struggle, sorrow, danger, and futility into work. Work is not a punishment. Adam and Eve had a job to do long before sin entered the picture. In fact, fulfilling the assignments God has given us to do on this earth is another way we are

13

meant to experience pleasure. You can see this in people whose job is not just a way to put food on the table, but who love the work they do. It seems easy to them and they enjoy it because they're anointed and graced for it.

The very first words man ever heard God say were, "Be fruitful and multiply, and fill the earth, and subdue it; and rule over the fish of the sea and over the birds of the sky and over every living thing that moves on the earth." (Genesis 1:28 NASB) That probably wouldn't have happened by floating around on clouds all day doing nothing while angels dropped grapes in their mouth! I think many have the mistaken idea that if things were perfect now like they were in Eden, we'd never work another day of our life, everything would be handed to us on a silver platter, and we'd just sail through life doing nothing but eat and be entertained, indulging our every whim. Sounds boring actually. I mean, if you're in desperate need of a vacation it probably sounds wonderful, but imagine if that alone was the epitome of your existence.

Genesis 2:5b (NASB), "The Lord God had not sent rain upon the earth, and there was no man to cultivate the ground." Evidently, cultivating the ground was going to be man's job. Sounds like work.

Genesis 2:15 (NASB), "Then the Lord God took the man and put him into the garden of Eden to cultivate it and keep it." Well, lookie there! God put him to work! In Eden!

Genesis 2:18b (NASB), "I will make him a helper suitable for him." If he was doing nothing, why would he need help?

Genesis 2:20a (NASB), "The man gave names to all the cattle, and to the birds of the sky, and to every beast of the field." I bet that was not a one day job. I bet they also had a lot of fun with it!

"But Jackie, I thought that having to sweat and work for your food and needs was a result of the curse!"

It was. Genesis 3:17b-19a (NASB), "Cursed is the ground because of you; in toil you will eat of it all the days of your life. Both thorns and thistles it shall grow for you; and you will eat the plants of the field; by the sweat of your face you will eat bread, till you return to the ground."

But wait. Didn't they *already* cultivate and keep the garden? So what's the difference? The difference is that work in an Eden environment always *works* to produce the desired outcome.

God's original intent was for man to live and work in and under the blessing initially pronounced over them in Genesis 1:28. The blessing is what empowered them to prosper. (Deuteronomy 8:18; Proverbs 10:22) Psalm 1 also shows us that a result of the blessing is that in whatever you do, you prosper. You succeed. What you're doing *works* in the sense of the word that means it has the desired outcome and operates or functions properly and effectively as it's supposed to. It's not just work as in the exertion of oneself to do a job, but it's work that *works*.

Imagine that kind of work. You have no trouble getting it to work, no do-overs because it didn't work right the first time, and no time or money spent fixing mistakes or problems. The end result meets or exceeds all expectations, bringing a very pleasurable sense of satisfaction. Was it still work? Yes, but that's what you call good, rewarding work!

Jesus knew all about that kind of work. He said in Matthew 11:30 (AMPC), "For My yoke is wholesome (useful, good — not harsh, hard, sharp, or pressing, but comfortable, gracious, and pleasant), and My burden is light and easy to be borne." TPT says it this way, "For all that I require of you will be pleasant and easy to bear." A yoke indicates you *do* have a job or assignment to carry out, but listen! As pointed out by the word "pleasant", this kind of work has pleasure attached to it. There's pleasure in *knowing* that your work is effective in producing the desired outcome, and there's pleasure in getting to enjoy the fruit of your labor. This is Eden-like work!

The work in Eden was not about meeting need. Their needs were already met, freeing their focus to zero in on their God-given assignments. It was only after sin, when humanity was disconnected from their true Source, that their work became all about meeting their own needs.

Jesus said in John 17:4 (AMPC), "I have glorified You down here on the earth by completing the work that You gave Me to do." Through Jesus' finished work, we can now be reconnected to the Source Who has already promised to meet all our needs according to His riches in glory. Taking care of our needs was part of the redemption plan, so we could live undistracted from fulfilling the work of our assignments. (Matthew 6:25-34; Philippians 4:19)

So what does all this talk about work have to do with pregnancy and birth? Well, birth is work. This is why it's called *labor*. Labor in the Eden environment is rewarding, wholesome, enjoyable, satisfying, and safe! However, it's still work. *Preparing* for birth is also work. If you want a fear free, Eden-like atmosphere to give birth in, as God originally intended and *still* desires for you, you will have to put in the work of cultivating and keeping the garden. This kind of experience will not just randomly happen without any intentional activity or involvement on your part. But remember, this is the prosperous and promising kind of work. This can be the best work you've ever had the joy to do!

As we all know, when sin introduced the curse, everything changed. Suddenly, for the first time, things didn't always work like they were designed to, at least not without a lot of toil and struggle to make it happen.

We've probably all, to some degree, done some work where nothing seems to go right. Maybe it took way longer than anticipated because you had to spend hours fixing problems and redoing the same thing rather than actually making progress toward completion. Everything cost more than it should have. To top it off, all that work then ended up producing less than desired or hoped for, resulting in disappointment. That's when frustration and even anger can begin to set in.

The original Hebrew words for "sweat" and "face" in Genesis 3:19, "by the sweat of your face", actually have a connotation of anger and vexation. The word "sweat" comes from a root word that means to be in terror or agitated as with fear. This is not just talking about physical sweating as a result of exerting your body. What would cause anger, frustration, vexation, and fear in your work? When the work doesn't prosper like it's supposed to, yet you're depending on it as your source to meet your needs, that's when fear comes with all its different faces like anger, frustration, and more.

According to Genesis 3:16, the curse also brought multiplied sorrow in pregnancy and birth. The word sorrow in this verse is also translated as grief, suffering, and pain. It means heavy and toilsome labor, the exact opposite of the kind of labor described in Matthew 11:30. It's also defined by Strong's Concordance as worrisomeness, coming from a Hebrew root word that can mean to grieve, vex, or even torture. The Gesenius' Hebrew-Chaldee Lexicon defines it as grief of mind and anger. Clearly, it's a word that refers to pain of either, or both, mind and body, all rooted in fear, just as we saw in the words "sweat of thy face". The modern English definition of sorrow includes grief, sadness, regret, or a feeling of deep distress caused by loss or disappointment. These definitions and translations taken together paint a precise picture of what kind of atmosphere and state of mind is a result of the curse. These were not the default settings of the birth environment!

You may have been taught that having to endure excruciating childbirth is simply a result of living in a fallen, broken world, a consequence of sin that we have to pay. "C'mon Jackie, this ain't no Eden!"

Foundational to everything discussed in this book is believing that yes, it is God's desire and best for us to give birth in an Eden-like atmosphere even today. He never changed His mind about the beauty, delight, and glory He designed us to experience in giving birth. You may initially think that sounds too good to be true, or even downright impossible. If you're thinking in only natural terms, that's exactly what it is. In order to believe this, we must see in the Word how God made a way, by faith in Jesus, for it to be possible once again.

If instead we choose to believe we do still have to suffer in childbirth because of sin and its curse, we need to ask ourselves some questions. Suppose it's true that every woman everywhere still has to bear "Eve's curse" with no way out. Suppose it's true that dreadful, I-want-to-die kind of birth really is about us paying the price for either Eve's sins, our own sins, or anyone else's sins. Suppose that suffering and torment in birth is God's plan and best for us. If so, why try to alleviate any of that suffering? Aren't you then fighting against God's will if you get an epidural or even a hip squeeze? If it's really somehow your punishment, shouldn't you just suffer the full force and brunt of it without any relief or comfort?

Not only that, but if indeed this is our God-given burden to bear, why do women's pain levels and difficulty in giving birth vary? Have some sinned more?

What about those who experience no pain, either by chance or supernaturally, both of which are entirely possible and do happen? Does this mean they never sinned? Have they reached flawless performance in God's eyes and managed to earn enough of His blessing and approval that He decided to remove the pain?

If our pleasure gives Him pleasure, as in Eden, then do we deny Him pleasure if we refuse to believe and receive the pleasure He planned for us in birth?

Are we fighting for a right to suffer, which gives Him no pleasure?

The truth is, we have all sinned and come short of the glory of God (Romans 3:23). We all needed a Savior. That Savior came, and when we take Him as our Savior, Jesus erases all our sins, meaning they can no longer be held against us or used as a reason for bad things happening to us. And yet, centuries of bad religion have poured guilt and condemnation on women, telling them that a horrific birth experience is just punishment and they must somehow deserve it.

Even in Jesus' day, the prevalent attitude was that if someone suffered tragedy or difficulty, it was because of their sin and they were being punished. In Luke 13:1-5, some had the faulty idea that the reason specific people had suffered an untimely death was because they had sinned more. Jesus corrected them by essentially putting everyone in the same pot, saying that unless *all* repent, all will perish. Again in John 9, He shook up the self-righteous belief system that used bad things happening to people as a measuring stick for how sinful they were. They didn't even question whether it was a sin issue that caused the man to be born blind. They just went straight to, "Who dunnit?" Was it because this guy sinned, or his parents? Jesus said, "Neither!"

If we have to pay for sins by suffering in birth, does that mean Jesus' payment for sin was insufficient? Was His suffering not enough?

Did He fail in His mission to redeem us from every aspect of the curse that sin brought into this world?

Does sin and its consequences still have more power than His precious blood?

Isaiah 53:4 in the AMPC says He carried our sorrows and pains of punishment, both physical and mental. Verse 11 of the same chapter says, "He shall bear their iniquities and their guilt [with the consequences, says the Lord]." Sorrowful, traumatizing childbirth was a consequence of sin and Jesus carried it away! Why then would we still think we have to pay the consequences too?

Isaiah 53:5 (AMP) says that the punishment required for our well-being, also translated peace, fell on Jesus. Again in Matthew 20:28 (AMP) we read that Jesus paid the price to set us free from the penalty or punishment of sin, which is anything that produces or is a result of fear and death, including all of the curse. (Romans 6:23)

When I accept and receive that *His* payment was the substitute for my own, there is nothing left that could or should be punished. I am *free* from the law of sin and death, and the curse of the law that says I must be punished, because *He* took *my* punishment! (Romans 8:2)

All throughout the Word you'll find words like redeem, reconcile, and restore. We need to ponder the prefix of all these words. "Re" means "back". In other words, it once was so, and can be or is being made so again. We must not only ask what we are redeemed from, but what are we reconciled to? From the beginning, God was working His plan to fully redeem us from the effects and power of sin and restore us back to that original place of freedom from everything the curse brought into this world, the worst of which was fear. There was no other reason for Jesus to come to earth, die on a cross, and rise again on the third day, but to make a way for us to get back into right standing with God, so that we could once again legally walk in the blessing He pronounced over mankind in Genesis 1:28.

Proverbs 10:22 (NASB) says, "It is the blessing of the Lord that makes rich, and He adds no sorrow to it." Yes, that word sorrow comes from the same root word as the word sorrow in reference to childbirth in Genesis 3. Because we are restored to the full blessing of the Lord, we can have a rich birth experience!

The blessing of the Lord creates conditions in which everything we do and believe profits and produces fruit, which has always been God's perfect plan, desire, and will for humanity. He is not ok with all our efforts being devoured (Malachi 3:11). He doesn't expect us to serve Him for nothing and actually rebukes those who say there is no profit or benefit in serving and obeying God (Isaiah 45:19; Malachi 3:13-15). In Jeremiah 23:32 He says He is against those who claim to speak for Him and yet don't furnish the people the slightest benefit, because their words are not actually from Him. This indicates that *His* word will always benefit and profit us. Isaiah 65:17-25 is also a beautiful picture of God's perfect will for people. As you read through it you'll notice it's not that they don't build, and plant, and work, just like in Eden, but that they actually get to reap and enjoy *all* the fruit of their labor, live long satisfying lives, and never labor in vain or bear children for calamity. They are *blessed* by the Lord and enjoying the blessing!

One of my favorite things about the story of Israel's time in Egypt is that there was always a vast difference to be seen between God's people and everyone else, even in birth. Exodus 1:7 says that Israel was fruitful and increasing, becoming exceedingly mighty. That sounds a lot like the blessing of Genesis 1:28 at work! Serving the childbearing women amidst this population growth were just two midwives. They were strong women who wouldn't bow to the pressures of government, society, or political correctness. They feared God above man. As a result they were summoned to give an account for why they had not killed all baby boys as commanded in order to control the population. Their response is fascinating! They said (paraphrased from several translations), "The Hebrew women are not like the Egyptian women. They are vigorous, and they give birth so easily and quickly that neither of us gets there in time!" This was not just a lie or excuse to get out of trouble. We know they were serving hundreds of thousands of women because at the time of the exodus there were six hundred thousand men alone, not counting women or children. With just two midwives, this means unassisted birth would have been common, and they were obviously not dying by the thousands as the world would like us to believe was the case for childbearing women before the introduction of medical interventions.

The word vigorous comes from a Hebrew root word that literally means "to live, to have life, sustain life, live prosperously, be alive, or be restored to life or health".... "They are not like the Egyptian women;

23

they are vigorous." They *lived* through childbirth, not died. They had easy, fast labors. Despite being wrongfully oppressed, they gave birth in the spirit of power, love, and a sound mind.

As defined by Webster's Dictionary, the word vigor "commonly implies active strength, or the *power* of action and exertion, *in distinction from* passive strength, or strength to endure".

So it wasn't just that they had the strength to endure a hard labor. There was power behind their exertion and efforts. Power is the ability to get results. They had the strength in spirit, soul, and body to actively and powerfully get the job done, not just passively endure whatever came their way.

How much more can we, fully redeemed and restored to God's blessing, living under a better covenant of grace, also believe and expect to give birth like that?

2 no fear involved

The number one element that determines whether we experience pregnancy and birth according to original intent is not whether we birth at home or in the hospital, whether we give birth vaginally or by c-section, whether we birth with or without intervention or medication, whether or not we are highly educated about our bodies and birth, or any other given issue.

While all the above and more can play a part, the greatest determining factor in whether we experience original intent in birth is whether or not fear is present.

The Lord's response to my question about what birth was like before sin sums it up just like that.

"There was no fear involved."

What was the greatest, most immediate, tangible consequence of sin's entrance into the world? Simply put, for the first time, fear became a part of mankind's existence.

It all began when Adam and Eve chose to believe a lie rather than the truth. But first, they had to hear the lie, a requirement which the devil was eager to fulfill, because he is the father of lies. Anytime he speaks there is deception in his words. There is *no* truth in him! (John 8:44)

Fear and faith operate by the same spiritual laws. They both come by hearing. Faith comes by hearing the Word of God which is the truth, while fear comes by hearing the contradictions to the Word, which are lies. (Romans 10:17)

If you are living controlled by fear, somewhere, somehow, you are hearing and believing a lie, which means you are also in unbelief about something God has said, because He cannot lie.

Wherever you pinpoint an area of unbelief you also identify an area of fear.

To deal with the fear, we must locate its source, which is the lie we are believing, to uproot it and replace it with the truth.

For Adam and Eve, the lie they believed was concerning God's character, which is what all the enemy's lies typically boil down to. The devil tempted them to think God had withheld from them something good and imperative for their completeness and happiness. That would make Him unjust and a violator of His own word (Proverbs 3:27). Satan also accused God of lying to them, questioning whether He really said what He did, or at the least, whether He really meant exactly what He said. If he could get Adam and Eve to wonder if God had purposely misled or lied to them, he could get them to doubt His love, because love doesn't do that.

In Deuteronomy 1:26-27, we see that the Israelites also lacked faith in the purity and integrity of God's character, which was one of the reasons they rebelled against Him. They thought God hated them and had brought them out of Egypt only to have them destroyed. They didn't believe He was love, and that faulty, twisted perspective gave birth to wrong behavior.

Similarly, in Matthew 25:14-30, evidently, the servant with the one talent had heard lies about his Master's character, believing He was hard and harsh, even though the first part of the story reveals otherwise. The first thing that false belief produced was fear, which again resulted in wrong choices and behavior (verse 25).

The greatest temptation of all time is to not believe the integrity of what God has said. Yielding to that temptation is the origin of every sin. (John 16:9; John 6:29) Sin subsequently introduces fear, and therefore, fear originates with not believing that God's character is perfectly pure.

I'm sure we've all heard commonly voiced conclusions about fear among both the world and believers such as:

"Fear is normal."

"It's ok to be afraid."

"Fear is not always bad."

"There's healthy fear and unhealthy fear."

"It's good to have some fear."

Despite the widely accepted belief that it's only natural to fear, science itself has proven that we are not created or wired for fear. Fear creates chaos in the body. We are wired for love[1], and our brain and body know it, because they will function at their highest peak of potential in a state of love. *Not* to fear is more intrinsic and native to us than *to* fear. While fear may be common, it is definitely not natural! We have to be taught and influenced to fear, and our enemy, the devil, is more than happy to do that, using lies.

Consequently, the large majority of people live in fear of *something*. It could be as extreme as the exaggerated and irrational fear of a phobia resulting in severe anxiety and panic attacks, or as minor as being afraid of what people think of their social media post. Rejection, lack, sickness, disease, and death are also everyday fears for many. Because fear is something every human deals with in some way, shape, or form, it's not surprising that some feel preaching a "fear not" message is to do nothing but lay impossible burdens and religious guilt on people. After all, "*everyone has fears*". Perhaps they'd agree that fear can be worked through, and you can "do it afraid", but that fear could actually be completely eliminated and overcome? To most, that just seems like unrealistic crazy talk.

The ultimate question is, however, whose word are you going to believe? Jesus repeatedly said, "Fear not!" He did not say, "Learn to manage your fear."

The thing is, if we don't understand what fear is, if we believe it's harmless, or if we continue to believe it's impossible to expel, we'll keep tolerating it instead of getting it and all its damage out of our lives for good.

"But Jackie, you can't just get rid of emotions."

Again, faith and fear are alike in that neither is merely an emotion, but rather, they are spirits. (II Corinthians 4:13; II Timothy 1:7) While they can both *produce* feelings and emotions, that's not actually what they *are*. As spirits, they are also not neutral.

Just as living by faith gives God access and opportunity to fill your life with good, operating in fear grants Satan access and opportunity to steal, kill, and destroy.

Without the presence of fear the devil is limited in his operations against us, just as without our faith God is limited in what He can do in and for us.

Faith and fear are both powerful forces that can bring things from the unseen into the seen. Faith is expectation of God's goodness, while fear is expectation of evil.

Fear, like faith, is a seed that will produce a harvest.

Job 3:25 is a great example of this, giving us insight into why the tragic events of Job's life occurred. The NKJV quotes Job as saying, "For the thing I greatly feared has come upon me, and what I dreaded has happened to me." Fear opens the door to the very thing you are afraid of, because God can do no mighty work in any area where He is not believed and trusted. (Mark 6:5-6)

I have watched this very principle play out in the birth space, when a mama was informed of the presence of a specific issue she had been hoping to avoid. She went from laboring calmly and peacefully to deeply distressed, begging in desperation for everything just to be over while crying, "This is exactly what I was afraid of!" While it wasn't something that compromised her baby and everything ultimately turned out well physically, because the thing she had so greatly feared came to pass, she still suffered in the mental and emotional realm. By yielding to the fear, which had already influenced some of her decisions before labor, what could have remained a thoroughly peaceful experience quickly became troubling.

That is certainly not to be taken as criticism of her. I don't believe she had a real understanding of the power of fear to bring to pass that which is feared. I loved and supported her through it the best I could, but it's a vivid example of the painful effects of fear, and why I want *you* to see the truth of this principle.

The story in Nehemiah 6 conveys another one of the objectives of fear. The enemies of God's people didn't take kindly to the fact that Nehemiah was rebuilding the walls of Jerusalem as directed by the Lord. They conspired together against him, even hiring prophets to falsely prophesy against him and the work. However, Nehemiah saw through the deception and recognized what they were trying to do.

Nehemiah 6:9 (AMPC), "For they all wanted to frighten us, thinking, 'Their hands will be so weak that the work will not be done.' But now strengthen my hands!" Verses 13-14, "He was hired that I should be made afraid and do as he said and sin, that they might have matter for an evil report with which to taunt and reproach me. My God, think on Tobiah and Sanballat according to these their works, and on the prophetess Noadiah and the rest of the prophets who would have put me in fear."

Fear wants to intimidate you into halting progress, productivity, and completion of that which God has called and instructed you to do. Fear, when received into the heart and acted on, is a paralyzing force.

Perhaps the greatest problem with fear is that, as I John 4:18 in the KJV points out, it's tormenting. The English definition of torment is severe mental or physical suffering, or extreme pain or anguish of body or mind. This sounds a lot like the definition of the word sorrow in Genesis 3:16 as discussed in chapter one. In truth, that's exactly what it is. When fear entered mankind's world, it came with sorrow and torment.

But what exactly were they so afraid *of* that could cause such great sorrow and torment? Looking at I John 4:18 in various translations gives us the answer to that. We find that fear is always related to punishment. It brings with it the thought of punishment; it involves the expectation of punishment. The NLT says, "If we are afraid, it is for fear of punishment." TPT goes on to say, "Whoever walks constantly afraid of punishment has not reached love's perfection", or as the AMP says, "has not grown into a sufficient understanding of God's love".

As we can see in Adam and Eve's case in the Garden, fear with the accompanying thought of punishment caused them to hide from and avoid the One who loved them most.

Nothing is more tormenting than fearful expectation of God's punishment and condemnation, wondering if He is against you, believing that He wants to keep distance between you, or that any of His thoughts toward you are for evil.

The truth is, Love sent Jesus, not to punish, but to *take* our punishment, so that we could live in complete peace, having our hearts nourished with His love! (Isaiah 53:5; John 15:9)

Romans 8:15 (AMPC), "The Spirit which you have now received is not a spirit of slavery to put you once more in bondage to fears." What type of spirit is it then? According to II Timothy 1:7, it's a spirit of power, love, and a sound mind.

Not only is fear itself bondage, but *all* bondage is always fear based. Yet, throughout the Word we find that God is all about *removing* heavy, oppressive, enslaving burdens and yokes that keep us bound.

Isaiah 61:1-2 and Luke 4:18 tell us that Jesus came to set oppressed captives free.

Galatians 5:1 says it was for freedom that we were set free, not to spend our lives in a prison of fear.

In any prison there are varying levels of security, with inmates who have differing privileges and freedoms *within* the prison walls. However, even the inmate with the most privileges is still not truly and completely free.

Sadly, many view life as a follower of Jesus in a similar manner. They don't really believe that He fully sets the captives free, but rather only makes their life in prison more manageable and endurable by giving them some privileges, as He sees fit, within their prison walls.

Friends, that's not how Jesus operates. II Corinthians 3:17 says that where the Spirit of the Lord is, who is the Spirit of *Love*, there is *freedom*. He doesn't do things halfway. He does all things astonishingly, overwhelmingly well! (Mark 7:37)

If Jesus has set us free from the bondage of fear, why does He still tell *us*, "Fear not"? What does it have to do with us?

When an inmate is pronounced free to leave the prison, they still have to use their own two feet to walk out the door and into their freedom. As they walk the streets in their newfound freedom, they still have to make a daily choice not to get entangled in something that will land them back in prison. Just because they have opportunity to go back to prison, doesn't mean they're not free, but they must choose not to take that opportunity; they must resist it.

Likewise, to walk in the freedom and victory Jesus won for us, we have a vital role of resisting our enemy and using the authority God has given us.

Galatians 5:1 (TPT), "Let me be clear, the Anointed One has set us free —not partially, but completely and wonderfully free! We must always cherish this truth and stubbornly refuse to go back into the bondage of our past."

God never takes away our freedom to choose, which is why we are greatly involved in remaining free from fear.

Fear comes not only by hearing but also believing a lie. Every time you hear something, good or bad, you still always have a choice whether to believe it. We get to choose whether we will yield to fear, or yield to God's truth!

John 14:27b (TPT), "Don't yield to fear or be troubled in your hearts— instead, be courageous!"

I believe a vital part of overcoming fear is understanding that just because a fearful thought enters your mind, that doesn't automatically mean the devil has been successful in causing you to fear. It's easy to feel, "I'm having fearful thoughts, so that must mean I'm in fear." If the devil can convince you to believe that you're in fear just because of a thought of fear he plants in your mind, you'll begin to act accordingly, which is obviously his entire goal. However, to be operating in fear, it must get in and fill your heart, not just your mind. Having a fearful thought alone does not mean fear is ruling over or controlling you.

Fear's knock at the mind's door doesn't mean you automatically possess it, or that you have to open the door and let it in. Like the old proverb says, "You can't stop a bird from flying over your head, but you can stop it from making a nest there." Not every thought that enters your mind is yours unless you receive it and make it yours. Fear can only take root in your heart when you begin to meditate on the lie to which you've been introduced. Matthew 6:31 (KJV) calls this "taking the thought". Taking the thoughts as your own is what actually gives them place in your heart.

As long as you resist, rather than receive, or take, every thought of fear the enemy plants in your mind, you have not yielded to fear, no matter how much you may feel it in your emotions! The devil's craftiness is such that when you've come to a solid understanding about what fear produces and why it's not ok to tolerate, he changes tactics and begins to try to trick you into fearing fear itself, or believing that every fearful thought means you've been had. But no! By the Spirit and grace of God, we are aware of his schemes and stop him from exploiting us in this way. You can be shaking in the flesh while standing strong in the spirit! As you continue to stand firm and resolute, the feelings of the flesh *will* follow your spirit.

Real evidence that you've taken a thought of fear, that it's actually in your heart and not just in your mind, can be found in your words. Continue reading Matthew 6:31, "Take no thought, *saying...*" You will start to hear the lie coming out of your own mouth, because out of the abundance of the heart the mouth speaks (Matthew 12:34). If fear is in there, it will come out. If faith is in there, it will come out.

Additional evidence of whether you've taken the enemy's thoughts of fear as your own is in whether you act on those thoughts. Consider again the parallels between how faith and fear work. James 2:17 tells us that faith without works, or being acted on, is dead. Verse 18 says that what we believe is revealed by our actions. If we are really believing the lie, we will act on it. We will make decisions based on it and let it steer our life. However, fear, just like faith, if not acted on, weakens and dies. You'll only act on what you truly believe.

Anger, inferiority, insecurity, anxiety, depression, worry, and even pride are all faces of fear. Worry is perhaps the most common of all, even worn as a badge of nobility, as if it makes you a good parent, or could actually improve the outcome of anything. Yet, it's nothing but negative meditation on contradictions to the Word.

Fear, in any and all of its forms, is a weapon of your enemy, and as such, you must fight back, putting up a resistance. You must prevent it from entering your heart even if it enters your mind.

I Peter 5:9a (NASB), "But resist him, firm in your faith."

So *how* do we resist?

According to II Corinthians 10:4, we, too, are armed with powerful weaponry for the overthrow and destruction of false arguments, theories, reasonings, and every prideful thing that raises itself up in defiance of the true knowledge of God. That includes every lying thought of fear.

All throughout the Bible we are given insight as to what our weapons are. Ephesians 6:17, among others, tells us that the Word of God is a weapon. Simply replacing the lies of the devil with the truth of the Word is powerful enough to effectively dismantle the plan of the enemy. Use the Word to cast down the enemy's thoughts, saying, "That's not my thought! My thoughts are true, honorable, right, pure, lovely, admirable, excellent and worthy of praise!" (Philippians 4:8) Say what God says about your situation!

I Timothy 1:18 reveals that prophecies are also given to help us fight the good fight. A good fight is one that you know how to fight, one that you have the necessary weaponry to fight, and one that you win. (I Timothy 6:12)

Praise, too, which is often expressed through thanksgiving, is a dynamic weapon that silences the enemy. (Psalm 8:2; Matthew 21:16) God inhabits, or dwells, where praise is! (Psalm 22:3)

The thing about the weapons God has given us is that they are guaranteed to work if and when we use them.

James 4:7 (AMP), "So submit to [the authority of] God. Resist the devil [stand firm against him] and he *will* flee from you." (emphasis mine)

The authority of God includes the authority of His Word. Submitting to His Word means to give it first place and have the attitude that, if the Word says it, then I believe it, I stand on it, and that settles it.

One thing His Word has said that we must submit to if we want to successfully resist the devil is that He has given *us* authority to trample on serpents and scorpions, and over all the power of the enemy, with nothing being able to hurt us. (Luke 10:19)

Submitting to that Word means we will say, "Yes, sir! Thank You! I take that authority and I will exercise it as You meant for me to!"

Ultimately, the most effective weapon against fear is love. It's *when* and *because* you believe that God is love, that you even have any valid reason to take Him at His word, give Him praise and thanksgiving, or submit to His authority by using the authority He has given you. Love is what gives us a reason to believe.

While the opposite of fear is typically thought to be faith, love is even greater than faith. Faith obviously plays a role, but according to Galatians 5:6, even faith only works by love. As my pastor so eloquently says, "Faith works when you know how much you're loved. Where there is no revelation of love, there will be no operation of faith."

I John 4:18a (AMP), "There is no fear in love [dread does not exist]. But perfect (complete, full-grown) love drives out fear."

Believing the Love makes it easier to resist temptation of any kind, but specifically that foremost, root temptation to not believe God. Because you know He loves you, you know He would never lie to you. You can be secure in that He'll take good care of you and do what you believe Him for, based on what He has said. When you believe He *is* love, you are able to trust that He is and does good only.

I think many feel that expelling fear once and for all couldn't possibly be as simple as believing God's love. "You don't understand. I've lived with this fear my whole life." It's such an overwhelming part of their daily reality they can't imagine becoming free from it could be that easy.

In II John 1:5-10 we are cautioned about not being content with the simplicity and ease of the power of love which Jesus taught. His core message was to walk in love (verses 5-6). There were those who wanted to run on ahead of that teaching instead of remaining in it, as though they wanted to move on to something new that felt deeper, or more exciting, extravagant, or eye catching in the flesh. In verse 10, John warns us concerning anyone who would either diminish or add to the teaching of Christ, the doctrine of love.

You might diminish it by minimizing its importance and power, or add to it by believing that other rules and beliefs must also be observed for true effectiveness. Either way, you'd be counting it as insufficient. Especially in the context of casting out fear, it's like saying that believing the love is too simple. There has to be something else.

Many are praying for God to take away their fear, while the answer is simply in believing how much He loves them. When people say, "God didn't take my fear away", they're actually saying, "I don't strongly believe that God loves me enough to do me good and not evil all the days of my life."

God wouldn't tell us not to fear without empowering us to carry out that instruction. Yet, when we push the responsibility back on Him by saying, "He didn't take it away", it's like accusing Him of unjustly expecting of us something He knows full well we don't have the power or ability to do. These are not the actions of someone who loves justice, has set the very standards for fairness, and whose very throne is founded on justice and righteousness. (Psalm 97:2; Psalm 89:14; Psalm 99:4; Proverbs 16:11) Therefore, we must believe that if He said it, He also empowers and equips us to do it.

At the same time, we must be clear that in and of ourselves we really *can't* do it. No amount of therapy, willpower, or positive thoughts apart from the grace and power of the Holy Spirit, the Spirit of love, can completely eradicate fear from the heart.

Fear is absent only where Love is present.

The revelation of love is the revelation of God's very nature and character, because He *is* love. Seeing God for who He really is, and then trusting in who He is, is what expels fear!

The primary way that a revelation of love comes is through the renewing of the mind as found in Romans 12:2. Renewing the mind means to exchange your thoughts, beliefs, and opinions for God's.

For example, II Timothy 1:7 says God has not given us a spirit of fear but of power, love, and a sound mind.

When we renew our way of thinking, we choose to believe that scripture, no matter what our feelings may be screaming. Many may call this denial of reality. "I'm not going to act like or say that I'm not afraid when I'm shaking in my boots! That's lying!" However, even God Himself, whom we are to imitate, calls those things which do not exist as though they did. (Romans 4:17)

We must remember that just because something is unseen in the natural, physical realm, doesn't mean it's not a reality. Hebrews 11:3 plainly tells us that everything we can see with our natural eyes was actually birthed from the invisible realm. How? Faith filled words, working by love, are the means by which everything came into being!

Very often when you decide to agree with what God says instead of what things look and feel like, you will be accused of being out of touch with or in denial of reality. This is because, for most people, their concept of reality only goes as far as what they can discern with their natural senses.

Luke 8:49-56 tells the story of a man named Jairus who asked Jesus to come heal his daughter who was dying. As they made their way to his home, someone met them to inform Jairus that his daughter had already died. *Still*, Jesus told Jairus, "Do not be afraid, only believe, and she will be made well!" (NKJV)

Many people today would call that denial of reality.

Is that what we are going to accuse Jesus of? No. He was simply looking at and aligning His thoughts, beliefs, and words with what is beyond the visible realm. And so can we!

We too have the same spirit of faith, believing, then speaking, and knowing we will have whatever we say in agreement with God's Word. (Mark 11:23; II Corinthians 4:13)

Hebrews 10:39 (TPT) says, "But we are certainly not those who are held back by fear and perish; we are among those who have faith and experience true life!"

The revelation of, and faith in, the love of God is what casts out fear, delivers from oppression, and destroys the power of the curse.

According to I Corinthians 13:8, it's *only* love that never fails. Therefore, it's only by and through love that all things become possible, including victoriously conquering fear for good. It's only by faith in the Love that we can do all things through Christ, including giving birth as God originally intended, without fear! (I John 4:8; Matthew 19:26; Mark 10:27; Luke 18:27; Philippians 4:13)

For birth to work at best capacity love must have full reign and be King.

The answer to fear can be summed up in these four famous words, "Yes, Jesus loves me!"

$\mathit{3}$ what about the pain?

In speaking of fear as it relates to pregnancy and birth, for many women, fear of the physical pain of childbirth is likely to be high on their list. In the middle of this message to fear not, it's like an unvoiced question that lingers in the air, "But, what about the pain?"

While pondering this question, the Lord dropped in my spirit, "There is nothing more painful than fear." He redirected the focus right back to the real source of suffering. The truth is, *fear* of pain hurts us more than the physical pain ever could.

Even so, every day women are undeniably experiencing physical pain in labor as well, and therefore I believe it's beneficial to directly address this topic and question. As you'll come to see, fear, mindset, environment, and more, all greatly affect our perception and experience of physical pain in birth.

As I mentioned in the previous chapter, we have to be taught and influenced to fear, and birth is one major area where the devil has worked overtime to do so. So extremely much so, that in itself should cause us to question why.

Why is he so dead set on trying to deter people from wanting to have children? What is the magnitude of the blessing he's attempting to rob us of?

How overwhelmingly beautiful is the blissful experience of birthing in peace and joy, in the very presence of God Himself? What facets of joy and blessing do children bring that nothing else can in quite the same way?

With the goal of preventing the realization of any of these good gifts from God, the devil influences society and culture to constantly pump out erroneous images and ideas of what birth is like. Most of us hear nothing but negative, dreadful stories anytime the topic of birth comes up. Movies depict women in labor on their backs, screaming bloody murder, with an "emergency" sure to pop up somewhere along the way. From social media, to grandmothers, to medical systems, to TV shows, almost everywhere we look pregnancy and birth are portrayed to be the most painful, miserable, and dangerous time of a woman's life. Is it any wonder why women are battling so much fear?

Dr. Grantly Dick-Read wrote in his book, "Childbirth Without Fear", that fear and the resulting tension are the cause of physical pain in childbirth for 95% of women. While I can't stand behind that number with all certainty, I do know that both science and the Word of God fully support the fact that, while fear causes more anguish that physical pain ever could, it also *does* increase *physical* pain.

Multiple scriptures clearly link fear with pain, revealing that fear actually precedes pain.

Psalm 48:5b-6 (NLT), "They were terrified and ran away. They were gripped with terror and writhed in pain like a woman in labor."

Isaiah 13:7b-8a (NLT), "Every heart melts, and people are terrified. Pangs of anguish grip them, like those of a woman in labor."

Jeremiah 6:24 (NLT), "We have heard reports about the enemy, and we wring our hands in fright. Pangs of anguish have gripped us, like those of a woman in labor."

Jeremiah 49:24 (NKJV), "Damascus has grown feeble; she turns to flee, and fear has seized her. Anguish and sorrows have taken her like a woman in labor."

Jeremiah 50:43 (NLT), "The king of Babylon has heard reports about the enemy, and he is weak with fright. Pangs of anguish have gripped him, like those of a woman in labor."

Notice that in all of these scriptures, the presence of fear is mentioned *before* the presence of pain.

From a scientific, physiological standpoint, if the physiological needs and requirements of a laboring woman are not met, her body will, at least to some degree, go into its emergency fight, flight, or freeze mode, releasing adrenaline and stress hormones, which undeniably increases pain levels and difficulty in giving birth. When this happens it tightens the pelvic floor, cervix and vagina, restricts dilation, decreases oxytocin production, restricts blood flow to the uterus, restricts oxygen to the baby which can increase heart rate decelerations, and can slow or completely stall contractions. It's a fear-tension-pain cycle.

While fear undoubtedly exacerbates every bit of physical pain, it's also important to point out that feeling physical pain in labor does not always automatically equate to the presence of fear. My last birth was my only unmedicated birth, and while I was not afraid at all, I did feel physical pain. Because I've learned and grown a lot since then, I believe even my experience of pain would be different now if I had it to do over again. Even so, it highlights the fact that the subject of pain in childbirth is a multifaceted issue; it's not strictly physical, nor strictly mental, nor strictly spiritual.

Healing and wholeness in spirit, soul, and body are a prerequisite to not being negatively triggered by the physical pain or intensity of labor.

While I know that some women do experience greater pain levels in labor than others, I also know that very often the women who seem to have a harder time with labor pain also have negative emotional, mental, or spiritual issues adding to the difficulty of the process.

Because fear and the resulting tension only increase physical pain and difficulty in giving birth, relaxation, achievable through surrender to the birth process, is absolutely essential for things to go as smoothly as possible and to experience the least possible amount of pain. Surrender and relaxation, however, are very difficult when your spirit or soul are not at complete rest and peace.

The truth of this can be clearly seen when you attend back to back births where one mom, who has done it multiple times before, is screaming and cussing, while the next, who is a first time mom, remains peaceful and calm, praying in the spirit, authoritatively speaking to her body and baby, and asking her husband to pray over her instead of yelling at him.

The truth is, our view of life, the state of our spirit and soul, what we have been taught, the impressions made on us, and our personal past experiences, all have shaped our thinking and affect our experience of pain or how we conceptualize the pain associated with birth. All factors as a whole, spirit, soul, and body must be considered in this question of what determines how a woman manages labor.

We certainly cannot chalk it all up to a woman's level of pain tolerance. The idea that some women are just tougher while others simply don't have what it takes is wrong. God did not intend that only some women would have the ability to birth their babies in strength and confidence and others not. Not only that, but what about women giving birth before medication was even an option? Did they somehow all have exceptionally higher pain tolerance levels than women today? No, unless pain tolerance is also determined at least in part by our mindset and expectations.

We must ask ourselves how our perception surrounding what is happening affects how strongly we feel, or interpret what we're feeling, as pain. We must ask ourselves what we are calling pain.

One of my favorite analogies to develop a more accurate image of what I mean by that is to compare the work of birth to physical fitness training and athleticism.

When someone works out intensely in the gym, although it may be difficult and exhausting, we don't typically think of them as being in excruciating pain. Their muscles are contracting, their bodies are working hard, they must be determined to give it all they've got, and they must maintain strong mental focus. You may even hear them grunt, shout, or otherwise express themselves vocally, but we *still* don't describe them as experiencing agonizing pain.

Take note, however. When doing something like intense physical fitness training that requires so much mental focus, strength, and stamina, there are multiple things that contribute to either the difficulty or the ease of getting the job done. When your workout is constantly interrupted, or you doubt your ability, or you're not properly fueled, or you think more about the difficulty than the reward, it gets that much harder doesn't it? You might even want to call it painful. But, when you have people believing in you and cheering you on, and you're able to maintain focus on both the task at hand and the reward, it's that much easier and less "painful". Think about it. Every little thing from the type of clothing you wear, the music you listen to, your food choices, hydration, and the mood of the room contributes to either the ease or difficulty of your fitness training. Labor and birth are no different!

In fact, I've often used the same words of encouragement I'd give someone in labor to motivate myself during a workout.

"If I can birth a baby, I can do this!"
"I can do anything for one minute!"
"Just breathe through it! Use your breath!"

Indeed, what's happening during labor really is much like a workout. The uterus, as a powerful muscle, is simply contracting, just like the muscle contracts when you flex a bicep. While giving birth is inarguably the most intense workout our body will ever do, it's not the same kind of pain as when there's a problem in your body. It's not pointless intensity, but rewarding work, the precious outcome of which far outweighs the effort put in!

The type of filter we place over the mind's eye is a powerful determiner in our experience of birth pain. We can think of labor and contractions as something that is happening to us, feeling as though we have no control, or we can choose to see it as a welcome tool that works in and through us to bring much desired results.

Now, you could have a mom who has not been adequately built up in spirit, soul, or body to be able to visualize and navigate labor pain in a wholesome, healthy way. She may be too unstable emotionally or mentally to conceptualize labor pain for what it really is, and any physical pain she experiences adds to her already existent trauma. In cases like this, the physical pain will probably be more strongly perceived and felt.

Another influence contributing to how much pain a woman experiences in labor is whether or not she's in an environment that supports and facilitates physiological birth. Because unmedicated birth does not necessarily equate to a truly natural, physiological birth, women who have an unmedicated, yet non-physiological birth, probably also have a heightened perception of pain. They may not realize that it could actually be much less painful if approached differently, and therefore come to have a misconceived idea of what natural birth is like. It's not natural to be continuously monitored, hooked up to IV's, limited in movement, restricted in what you can eat or drink, be required to answer questions, do paperwork, engage in conversation, and have a variety of people put their hands inside you all throughout the day, all while in labor. I'm not saying all these things are inherently evil or wrong, but they do not facilitate natural, physiological birth, which generally tends to be less painful than disturbed birth. (more on that in chapter five)

None of these scenarios are meant as criticism of anyone or their birth choices, but to point out that there are multiple factors determining the level of pain you feel.

For a well rounded discussion of labor pain, I must also tell you that yes, it is possible for women to give birth without any pain at all, even without drugs. It's not just a fluke of nature either, but a result of focused faith that has been intentionally built up in this specific area. I know several people personally, along with having heard and read many other stories, who have experienced minimal or no pain at all in birth. I also personally know someone who had an orgasmic birth. "What?? You mean birth can feel good? It can be fun and enjoyable?" One thing's for sure, if all we've heard and have experienced regarding birth is fearful, negative, and painful, it takes a lot of mind renewal and replacing lies with truth to believe anything else is possible.

A common thread in births with decreased or little to no pain is, as mentioned previously, surrender to the process. This is, again, something that involves spirit, soul, and body, because surrender is tied to trust, which is tied to love.

In speaking with, observing, and reading about women who have experienced pain free birth, I've come to understand that birth without pain is still powerfully intense. As I watched one particular mother labor painlessly, she looked and sounded a lot like other laboring women do, albeit in a calm manner, because even pain free birth is still work! She later said she'd had the opportunity to yield to thinking of what she was feeling as pain, but she chose not to. It reminds me again of the workout similarity, where it might also be easy to call what you're feeling pain if you chose to. However, when you think of it as working power and ability, it feels more like progress than pain. Also, as in a workout, being extremely focused and maybe even vocalizing, doesn't mean the person is in excruciating pain.

Quite honestly, the physical pain or intensity of labor alone is rarely what causes mothers to feel they're at the end of their rope, or what would cause trauma and suffering in the true sense of the word. That may be hard to believe, and understandably so, because for so long the pain of natural labor has been so widely portrayed as the most torturous event of our life, while drugs and artificial intervention are seen as the heroes swooping in to rescue us from anything natural. However, if it's true that it's the actual physical pain of unmedicated labor that is most awful and traumatizing, how is it possible that although I've attended significantly more physiological, natural births than medicalized ones, most of the trauma I've witnessed has been in the medicalized births? It doesn't add up.

The truth is, trauma is usually a result of either being treated wrongly, undesired intervention, or intervention that was unexpected or ill-prepared for.

We have been so largely conditioned to think that not feeling anything in birth is the better, easier way, that we choose to have feelings deemed as bad turned off, but in so doing we also turn off a lot of the pleasure and euphoria of birth. We've so embraced this idea that modern technology and interventions make it possible to avoid all the discomfort and difficulty of giving birth that we willingly, albeit unknowingly, accept all kinds of alternative pain and a new set of problems that otherwise wouldn't even exist.

Everyone has heard about the pain of contractions and the ring of fire, but who has heard about the pain and stress that interventions which are supposed to make everything better can cause?

Who exaggerates the pain of placing epidurals, or the pain of increased postpartum depression, persistent back pain, and headaches thanks to drug usage? Who magnifies the pain of restricted movement, or the pain of placing catheters? What about the pain of increased rates of tearing, episiotomies, forceps and vacuum extractions associated with the use of many common interventions? Who talks about the pain of having an IV placed while simultaneously trying to maintain focus through a contraction? Who emphasizes the longer, more painful recovery after a c-section? What about the pain of difficulty to bond with and breastfeed your baby because the natural ebb and flow of hormones has been interfered with? What about the pain of being told what you can and cannot do, which serves to decrease your trust in and ability to listen to and follow your body's divine design? What about the pain of a baby born with broken bones due to an unnecessarily rough, rushed delivery? What about the unnatural pain of unnatural contractions? What about the pain of being pressured into things you don't want? What about the pain of constant, unnecessary vaginal checks and pressure to make progress? What about the pain of apologizing to your newborn baby that you can't hold them because you're violently shaking and vomiting as a reaction to certain drugs?

You may call this fear mongering, but how could this be fear mongering any more than telling someone how terrible natural labor is?

Now please don't misinterpret me to be stating that all pain medication and medical intervention is always bad, or that the only way God intended for women to give birth is always and completely naturally, as if it's a rule. This is not the case at all. First of all, it should be, and is, the birthing woman's choice. However, if only one side of the story is told or seen, it affects her ability to make the best choice for herself.

There are times I've been very thankful for medical intervention, agreeing that it was the right choice considering the circumstances, and believing it really would help the situation rather than hurt it. For example, if mom has already been laboring for days and is near the point of total exhaustion, sometimes an epidural is just what she needs to get some rest, gather her strength, and finish the job, making it possible to avoid a c-section. Every birth is fluid and unique, and we cannot make one-size-fits-all rules or blanket statements about how everything should or should not be done, leaving no room for being led by the Holy Spirit. Those times when drugs actually are life saving are also a whole different ballgame.

The point is that opting for every intervention and drug you think will make birth easier for fear of what is natural, choosing to have your body's feelings completely turned off, is not guaranteed to truly make your birth experience better or even pain free. It doesn't come without its own price.

I love the fact that Jesus knew something about labor and birth. It makes me wonder if perhaps He witnessed the births of His siblings. Interestingly, as far as I can tell, He is the only one in the whole Bible who specifically points out how a mother immediately forgets what she went through thanks to the overwhelming joy that comes with welcoming her new baby into the world! (John 16:21) It seems that particular aspect of birth stood out to Him more than anything else. It's as though it ministered to Him as a distinct, tangible illustration of the joy that He too would one day experience after laboring to give new birth to us through His death, burial, and resurrection. We were the joy set before Him, and He always kept His eyes fixed on the prize!

The unparalleled joy of giving birth is the closest thing to the joy of the Father's heart and all of Heaven when one person is spiritually born again. To think that we as women have been given this gift and opportunity to taste that joy is nearly incomprehensible!

Once again, the immediate joy after birth is a whole person experience, not only mental, emotional, or spiritual but also physical. Beta-endorphins are your natural pain relief hormones similar to drugs like morphine, acting on the same receptors in the brain. These beta-endorphins will increase all throughout a properly supported labor and reach their peak immediately after delivery. A combination of beta-endorphins along with very high levels of oxytocin and prolactin create what is often described by mothers as a euphoric state right after birth. We often call it a birth high! That hormonal high is also playing a very important role in facilitating bonding with your baby and kicking off an easier breastfeeding journey.

To be fair, however, I must also tell you that you will likely not experience the full flow and benefits of these amazing hormones in a labor and birth that is medicated or subject to multiple interventions. Most studies have found a sharp drop in endorphin levels with use of epidural or opioid pain medication.[2] Additionally, no synthetic hormone is able to entirely replicate a natural one. For example, while Pitocin®, which is synthetic oxytocin, can cause contractions just like oxytocin does, natural oxytocin can change your perception of labor pain and make you feel good about your contractions. Pitocin®, however, cannot do that, because it doesn't cross the blood-brain barrier.[3] This is why many women have reported pitocin-induced contractions to be much more painful than natural, spontaneous contractions.

Understandably, we all want the easiest way, which is not automatically a decidedly bad thing. In fact, it was one of the incentives Jesus offered in His invitation to come to Him in Matthew 11:28-30. He said His way is the easy, light way.

In Proverbs 13:15 we find it's actually the way of the *unfaithful*, meaning they do not remain true to original intent, that is the hard way. (AMP)

Seek out and become fully persuaded of God's original intent *for you* in your birth experience. Remain faithful to it, and that will be the easiest, least painful way possible for you to give birth!

4 satisfaction vs. disappointment

My first pregnancy found me highly uneducated and uninformed about birth, not only because it was a subject that wasn't very openly discussed while growing up, but also because I didn't do any personal research. Obviously having no experience, and never really having heard that there even was anything *to* research, I just blindly accepted hospital policies and whatever doctors said, assuming that since they were the professionals they knew better than I and surely would do what was best. I also didn't know that legally I had a choice in every single matter, but presumed there was some untold rule that you had to do what they said or there could be trouble.

The biggest thing I really had going for me was faith in God. I may have been naive, but at least I was not afraid. Although we didn't know much to ask for, the few things we did specifically ask and believe God for, like which doctor we wanted to be on call, He faithfully brought to pass.

This birth had a lot of interventions. I was given Pitocin ® for augmentation of labor, an early epidural, was kept in bed the whole time, my water was broken artificially, baby was continuously monitored, an episiotomy was performed, and more. There was also no such thing as delayed cord clamping or immediate skin to skin with my baby after birth. Despite all this, everything worked out amazingly well including breastfeeding, especially considering what I now know about how often those types of interventions and practices can produce complications and interfere with bonding and feeding. My entire labor was only twelve hours start to finish which I later learned is also not very typical for that type of first birth.

Although it was a highly medicalized labor with said unnecessary interventions, I didn't feel traumatized at all, largely because I thought that was normal birth and because of the absence of fear. However, deep down inside there was a sense of disappointment, like a quiet, inner knowing that it could have been different or better. At this point in life though, that was very easy to just dismiss into a deep dark corner.

The pregnancy and birth of baby number two was not much different in terms of intervention or the lack of research on my part, other than a little digging I'd begun to do into vaccines. I basically went along with whatever I was told, which included an induction for the sole reason that I'd passed forty-one weeks gestation. Again, the birth went remarkably smoothly and quickly considering the interventions and the fact that we discovered she was in a posterior position up until right before delivery when the nurse managed to turn her. From the time I started feeling contractions to birth took only four and a half hours, definitely not a common occurrence with an induction! Because I did not get another episiotomy recovery was also easier. This time I actually said from the beginning that I wanted an epidural, unlike with my first when I had initially wanted to try going without. In my first labor it was pushed for early on, citing how bad things were going to get, so I consented before I even felt I needed it, at only three centimeters dilated to be exact. The second time around, upon a cervical exam immediately following epidural placement, I was already dilated to seven centimeters.

The epidural worked so well that I felt absolutely nothing when she was born, not even the release of pressure I'd felt with my first. Had they not held her up for me to see I wouldn't have known she was out. It may sound odd to some, but that was disappointing. I didn't like it. I'd felt less physical pain during the actual delivery than with my first, and yet that sense of disappointment deep down was compounded, stronger than the first time. Even getting induced was like a damper on the event because it felt like part of the adventure was taken away. However, again, everyone was healthy and happy, and these feelings were fairly easy to push away and ignore.

Then came pregnancy number three! There was a little more space between babies two and three then there'd been between one and two. By this time, I'd actually begun to do some of my own research rather than just believing whatever I was told whether I liked it or not and whether it was evidence based care or not. My quest to dig deeper was also influenced by the fact that my sister who was pregnant with twins was planning a home birth (which she achieved, all of them safe and sound). I now also had some personal experience under my belt, which served to help me see things I wanted and liked versus things I didn't. This time I made sure to go over my birth preferences with my doctor well ahead of time. I didn't want to have to lie down in bed, but rather remain mobile, choosing positions most comfortable to me. I did not want an epidural or episiotomy, or have my water broken artificially. Despite her verbal agreement to everything I had discussed with her, when it came down to it, the request for no episiotomy was the only thing that was honored.

Although everything in her 41-week bio physical profile checked out perfectly, I was again being pressured to get induced for the reason that my baby was apparently nearing nine pounds. While the pressure swayed me to consent to scheduling an induction, with a little more time to think it through, I ultimately decided against it. Thankfully, I ended up going into labor spontaneously in the wee hours of the same morning I had planned to call in to cancel the induction.

Upon arrival at the hospital in early labor, immediately after check-in I was told to lie down, despite explaining that my doctor had agreed I didn't have to. Well, apparently I had to wait until she finished the surgery she was performing and could approve in person. Once she finally arrived I immediately took up my case with her, to which she replied that in order to get out of bed and be mobile they'd have to monitor the baby internally, meaning she would have to break my water to insert the monitor. While she had mentioned internal monitoring previously, she'd never explained what that would entail, namely, the artificial rupture of membranes. I also didn't know that attaching an internal monitor is done by piercing the top layer of baby's scalp to screw it in place. While all of this was not what I'd wanted, I decided to compromise if that meant being able to get out of bed. Breaking the sac of water will often greatly intensify contractions and removes the cushioning it provided, but the doctor only told me this after the fact. That proved to be the case for me. It seemed like contractions went from zero to sixty immediately, so much so that I didn't even *want* to move and ended up staying in the bed, the very thing we'd done all of this to avoid! To top it off, the internal monitor wasn't even working properly. Everyone knew I'd said I didn't want an epidural, but soon started bringing it up anyway, warning that if I waited too much longer, it would be too late. It sucks to have to make decisions while in labor, especially when you thought you'd already made them. I flip flopped for a while before I finally consented, largely because nothing else was really going the way I'd envisioned either, only to find out that the anesthesiologist was in surgery and I'd have to wait! I was then given an intravenous drug that made me feel so sleepy and drunk that I'd forget where I even was and that I was having a baby, until a contraction would hit. I hated it and was crying to my husband that I didn't want to be asleep when my baby was born! Thankfully, it wore off pretty quickly. Finally, the epidural was placed, and while it took off the edge it never took full effect like it had in my previous labors. By that time, however, I was close to pushing and baby girl was born shortly after, weighing in at only seven pounds and six ounces, a far cry from what I was told as an attempt to convince me to be induced. Again, it was only an eight hour labor start to finish, my baby was healthy and strong, I had no abnormal physical damage, and yet I was deeply disappointed. I wouldn't describe it as trauma. I felt more mad and disappointed than wounded and traumatized. Not long after, I told my husband, if we ever had another baby and if the birth was to be like what I knew I was capable of and actually desired, it would not be in a hospital.

Perhaps your conclusion after all that is, "Well, if you hadn't raised your expectations so high or hadn't opposed routine practices and just gone with the flow like your first two births, then it wouldn't have so greatly affected and disappointed you." Aiming low due to fear of getting hurt or being disappointed may, to some, seem like the easiest route of thought that makes most sense. Had I done that, however, I would never have had one of the most glorious, deeply satisfying experiences of my entire life, which was my fourth birth. It was everything I'd known all along was somehow possible! The icing on the cake was that she was our rainbow baby whom we had stood and believed for, refusing to give up or give in. This kind of satisfaction comes only from the Lord and His perfect design. It's also a healing balm. You see, it came largely from being loved with the Lord's love through the people who surrounded me at that birth. They made every effort to accommodate my desires and cater to my needs as an individual. They put my comfort and convenience before their own. They treated me as Jesus would. I didn't have to worry about whether they were truly for me or against me, and whether I'd have to fight unnecessary, distracting battles while in labor.

I want to challenge you not to ignore any sense of disappointment you may have in regard to either a past birth experience, a medical care provider, or even attitudes and mentalities surrounding pregnancy and birth that you've been exposed to. Even if you've never yet been pregnant, you may feel as though something is "off" about the way some people talk and act about pregnancy and birth, or about certain birth practices and maternity care models. While it took me longer than it needed to, I'm thankful I listened before it got to the point of trauma. You don't have to first be traumatized. Just pay attention to the softer voice that sometimes sounds like disappointment.

Disappointment or dissatisfaction is the very evidence that there is more; that you are called to a higher level and way of thinking. It may be tempting to go with the line of thinking that tells you not to get your hopes up too high, but trying to protect yourself from disappointment by aiming low won't work.

It reminds me of a cartoon illustration I once saw depicting an artist creating a painting. The caption reads, "Lots of people will tell you how difficult it is to be an artist", with some idiot on the sideline yelling, "You'll starve!" The next scene has the same artist miserably working a desk job with a taskmaster behind him yelling, "Work!" The second caption reads, "But nobody tells you how difficult it is *not* to be an artist."

Many will tell you how impossible, costly, and difficult it is to pursue God's vision and plan for birth, but they won't tell you how costly, limiting, and difficult it is to pursue anything *but* that vision. He has given us an innate gift in that we are designed by Him to be able to give birth with peace, joy, and pleasure. Our inner being longs for and urges us to reach out and take that gift, but we often allow ourselves to be talked out of it, whether through analytical reasoning, past negative experience, or even current world views and societal pressures. You can back out of what you know you are born for and capable of out of fear that it won't work and you won't make it, but experiencing the heights you were created and designed for is the only thing that will satisfy you and protect you from disappointment. The thing is, what you are born, wired, and designed for won't just go away if it's not developed, satisfied or fulfilled. The gifts and callings of God are irrevocable (Romans 11:29).

Because perfection is the only thing that contains zero disappointment, perfection and satisfaction always go together. You might roll your eyes at that thinking, "Great. That means it's impossible to be satisfied, because don't you know nothing is perfect?"

First of all we need to address the lie that nothing is perfect. It *is* true that not *everything* is perfect, but there are pieces of perfection all around us. It's our definition and perception of perfection that is often faulty.

You'd be surprised at how much can be found in the Word about the existence of perfection when you start looking for it. You may argue that the word perfect is just an old King James way of speech, as many newer translations rather use words like mature or complete. But that's just the thing. Words like fullness, completeness, maturity, and wholeness actually more accurately define perfection than what we typically think of today when we hear the word.

We think perfect means flawless, even unrealistic, because much of what is called perfection in the pretense of today's world *is* unrealistic.

Yet, real, as opposed to fake, is a piece of perfection because it's satisfying. People crave and desire authenticity. That's why religion doesn't satisfy, because it's not the real thing. We must differentiate between unrealistic, stressful, legalistic perfectionism and Biblical, pure perfection.

We must renew our minds to the fact that Biblical perfection does exist and is attainable. The Bible definition of perfection is anything that truly satisfies, completes, and fulfills. It contains no disappointment and doesn't leave you wanting. Anything tainted by sin or evil is incapable of this, so we don't have to worry about being satisfied with the wrong things. We're not talking about short-lived, fleeting moments of fleshly gratification, but real, lasting satisfaction.

According to James 1:17, anything that comes from above, from Heaven, is perfect. Jesus Himself instructed us in Matthew 6:10 to pray that God's will be done on earth as it is in Heaven. Our hearts are actually drawn to perfection because every piece of perfection is a taste and glimpse of the atmosphere of Heaven, the nature and presence of God!

Where can we find some of these pieces of perfection? We see them in the pure innocence and joy of a baby's laughter, or the beauty and stunningly intelligent design found in nature. Love, peace, and all the other fruit of the Spirit is so perfect that there can be no law against it (Galatians 5:22-23). Full assurance of the will of God is a piece of perfection. James 1 speaks repeatedly of perfection - perfect gifts, perfect completeness, and the perfecting law of liberty. Maturity is also spoken of as perfection. Fruit doesn't come without maturity, so in essence, fruit too, is a piece of perfection. In II Chronicles 16:9 we find it's possible to have a heart that's perfect toward God. As a born again believer, one third of you is already perfect, born of incorruptible seed. (I Peter 1:23)

Psalm 19:7 and Psalm 18:30 tell us that the Word of God and the ways of God are perfect. Therefore, when you put your trust in what you've heard from Him, you'll never be disappointed! That's why it's so satisfying to live by faith in response to a Word from God. Whatever the Word of the Lord is to you, for you, and about you, that is the perfection that will satisfy you.

Absence of disappointment is evidence of perfection.

Because they are opposites, looking at what it means to be disappointed also helps us better understand what it means to be satisfied. Disappointment is the outcome when you thought something would be better, more fulfilling and pleasurable. It comes as a result of unmet expectation. It may feel like something is missing, or just somehow seems "off". Sometimes you can even be disappointed in something good, because although it was good, it wasn't quite perfect and didn't quite satisfy. You might even feel somewhat guilty for feeling disappointed, because after all, it wasn't that horrible. And yet, it feels like you had to settle.

In 2017, I had a dream in which I was getting ready for a wedding in a room with what seemed to be professional event coordinators or assistants. Upon first putting on my gown, the top of the dress was so sheer I needed to wear something underneath, which didn't quite match or look as white as the rest of the dress. Next, the dress was about one size too big. The fit was so slightly off that I knew if we had to make it work without any changes we could, but I was still a little disappointed and thought it should fit better. I wondered if we couldn't at least pin it or *something*! My assistant just brushed it off, downplaying that it didn't fit right. It was also too late for alterations because it was the day of the wedding. Last but not least, my assistant partially ripped the dress as she pulled off the price tag. I was surprised that she didn't even seem to care, figuring no one would see it anyway. She made a comment about the price as in surprise that I'd gotten such a good deal, and her carelessness almost seemed to stem from her thinking that the dress was not super expensive anyway so it didn't really matter. The entire time I was gazing at myself and the dress in a large mirror, deeply reflective. A dominant thought in the dream was that you should always try the dress on well ahead of time in order to make sure it fits just right and you have time to make any alterations if necessary.

Alterations are made on something valuable enough to be worth tweaking to perfection, not something cheap. The danger in being on the receiving end of a good deal is the temptation to treat it casually, as though it's cheap and insignificant. In birth, we are on the receiving end of a very good thing that sometimes simply needs a few adjustments to be *perfected*.

How do you know when something needs to be adjusted? If I only compare imperfect with imperfect, it may seem ok or good enough. However, by gazing intently into what is perfect, the mirror of the Word of God, I will notice when something is even just slightly off, even things that those who are supposed to be the professionals may minimize or think lightly of. In fact, often that's the only way I'll be able to identify something unsettling or even detrimental. (James 1:17, 23-25)

Sometimes people downplay a lack of excellence and perfection both in birth and elsewhere with an "it's good enough" attitude. They may even criticize you for wanting more, thinking you're too demanding, picky, or selfish.

"Why can't you just be happy with what everyone else is happy with?"

"You got the dress for a good deal - so what if the fit's not perfect or there's a little tear. No one will notice! It's no big deal! It doesn't have to be perfect!"

But why the disappointed feeling then, like you have to settle?

You see, because I'm born again of incorruptible, perfect seed, my spirit is recreated in perfection and therefore desires for that perfection to overtake and permeate every aspect of my life.

If you're still having trouble picturing perfection as a tangible reality, imagine someone designing and decorating a room. The process may look and sound a lot like:

"Let's try this. No, put that chair over here. Move that painting a little to the left. We need to change the wall color. Hmmm, something's still missing. Those styles are clashing. Add this pop of color. Move that piece to the right." On and on *until*….

"There! That's *perfect!!*"

And with those words, you know they are satisfied!

Whether in design, birth, or anything else, what satisfies one person may not satisfy another, and that's ok. In fact, that's exactly how it should be, because we are not meant to all be crammed into one and the same box.

A history enthusiast will not be satisfied listening to a science teacher.

Baby food will not adequately nourish and satisfy an adult. Likewise, a baby cannot receive suitable nourishment from adult food, because they cannot digest it. Even though they are both consuming what is good for them individually, switched around it would be detrimental, even dangerous. Does this make either one of them less than the other? Absolutely not!

In the same way, one type of plant will grow and thrive in a specific environment, nourished and satisfied with a specific diet, while another plant in the exact same environment with the same diet would not do well at all. Yet, there's nothing wrong with either one of them.

No one should be shamed, discredited, or condemned for the birth preferences that satisfy them personally. The only problem is in wanting to force others to be satisfied with the same things they are satisfied with, or purposely preventing others from having a satisfying birth experience.

It's not about hospital birth versus home birth, medicated versus drug free labor, vaccinated versus unvaccinated, circumcised versus intact, or the million other things used by the devil to try and pit us against each other. It's about having the freedom to hear from God and choose to follow the path of perfection He has for you personally, as a unique individual, which will leave you satisfied to your core. It won't be the same for everybody, because nobody's the same.

Now, you may be wondering, isn't it selfish to think so much about my own satisfaction? Again, that depends on our definition and perception of satisfaction. Selfishness itself doesn't satisfy. We all know that when our motive behind something has been selfish, even if we ultimately got what we wanted, it didn't hold the same satisfaction as when our motive is faith and love.

When you are motivated by faith in God's love for you, acknowledging the desires He Himself put in you, that's not selfish. In fact, if you refuse the goodness of God because you're afraid it might make you look selfish, that is actually where the self-centeredness lies, because your focus is more on your image than on giving God the pleasure of seeing His child happy, blessed, and fulfilled.

However, don't just take my word for it. Look at what God says about satisfaction.

In Isaiah 32:6 (NASB), God calls them fools who keep the hungry unsatisfied and withhold drink from the thirsty.

To *keep* someone unsatisfied indicates that not only do they themselves not give them what they need, but they also prevent them from getting it anywhere else. The King James translation of this verse reads, "make empty the soul of the hungry".

In Matthew 23:13 and Luke 11:52, Jesus called out the religious rulers for hindering and disallowing those who desired to enter the Kingdom to do so. The Pharisees not only had no hunger for God themselves, they also tried to prevent others who were hungry from being satisfied. According to Psalm 146:7, withholding from the hungry is linked to injustice.

Is it not injustice to withhold the satisfaction of a mother's needs in birth? It it not unjust if she feels like her soul has been made empty? Doesn't the Word say, "Do not withhold good from those to whom it is due, when it is in the power of your hand to do so?" (Proverbs 3:27 NKJV)

Not only does God have a problem with people being held from satisfaction by those who don't care about the satisfaction of another, He repeatedly speaks of the satisfaction He Himself gives on earth.

Psalm 104:13b (AMPC), "The earth is satisfied and abounds with the fruit of His works."

Psalm 103:5 (TPT), "You satisfy my every desire with good things."

Psalm 65:4b (AMPC), "We shall be satisfied with the goodness of Your house, Your holy temple."

Psalm 63:5a (NLT), "You satisfy me more than the richest feast." TPT reads, "The anointing of your presence satisfies me like nothing else. You are such a rich banquet of pleasure to my soul."

Psalm 36:8 (NKJV), "They are abundantly satisfied with the fullness of Your house, and You give them drink from the river of Your pleasures."

Clearly the Lord has our satisfaction in His heart and on His mind. He knows that apart from Him and outside of His path it's unattainable, so He's not worried that we'll find it in something else. Our hunger to be truly satisfied will lead us to Him and His plan for us.

So, what kind of birth experience are you hungry for? Be honest with yourself. Don't ignore any telltale signs of disappointment, as subtle as they may be. Pursue the intimacy with God that will lead you to the revelation of the perfect place, the perfect words, and the perfect people for *your* birth space. Then, watch His perfection satisfy you as only it can!

5 physiology of sex & birth

One of the most enlightening ways I have found to communicate the body's physiological design and needs in labor and birth is to call attention to the parallels between birth and sex.

A large reason why they have many physiological similarities is that birth and sex are both controlled by the same part of the brain.

The brain stem, also sometimes called the primitive or reptilian brain, governs basic functions, drives, and instincts such as heart rate, sleeping, breathing, digestion, balance, self-preservation, reproduction, and birth. It also distinguishes between familiar and unfamiliar, and detects threats. Notice that all these functions, drives, and instincts come naturally without you having to think them through, or consciously make them happen. You don't have to learn to sleep. Sexual attraction doesn't have to be taught. Birth too, just like breathing or sex, is something your body instinctively, by default, knows how to do!

What also ties birth and sex together is that neither is ever just about what happens physically, despite that the majority of what society portrays and emphasizes about either birth or sex is all in the physical realm. Sex is magnified to be all about the physical pleasure of the moment, with no regard to its emotional, mental, or spiritual effects. Birth is magnified to be all about physical pain and what might go wrong physically, with no regard to how the physical might be affected by the mother's state of mind, emotions, or peace, and vice versa. The so called dangers of birth are highlighted at every turn, while almost anything seems to pass as safe sex, as long as you're using contraceptives and protection against disease.

The truth is, what really makes birth either safe or dangerous is the same thing that makes sex either safe or dangerous. The safety of birth and sex depends on the setting, people's motives, consent, love, intimacy, freedom of choice, protection, and guarding of the heart. Danger in both birth and sex presents itself in the use of force, coercion, manipulation, fear, wrong timing, wrong people, lack of intimacy, and prematurity.

To really have this hit home we need to understand that, by physiological design, for both sex and birth to work optimally and be as easy and enjoyable as possible, they physiologically require the same settings and conditions. Many of the exact same things that make the baby also get the baby out. The same hormones are released, you have the same needs for intimacy, you use the same parts of your body, and you even make much of the same sounds and movements. Yet, ironically, for the majority, birth is expected to work and be satisfying in an environment and under conditions that sex never would.

The way in which the brain stem controls both birth and sex is by governing the release and flow of the hormones necessary to facilitate these events. These include oxytocin, the master labor hormone, as well as endorphins, melatonin, and others. A high, unhindered, uninterrupted flow of oxytocin is vital to having the easiest, quickest, and most enjoyable experience both in birth and sex.

In labor, oxytocin is what stimulates the uterus to contract, which is just as vital for delivery of the placenta and protection against hemorrhage as it is for the delivery of the baby. Oxytocin is also the primary hormone that supports bonding with your baby, and is responsible for milk ejection. Oxytocin is called the love hormone and creates those warm, fuzzy, cuddly, mushy feelings of love, as well as feelings of well-being and health. When released outside the birth space it may cause you to feel sociable and enjoy connecting with people. Oxytocin is only released in calm settings and when love is present, like when enjoying good conversation or a good meal with people you love, or when having good, safe sex.

When oxytocin is flowing optimally, endorphins, also known as feel-good or happy hormones, are released. Endorphins are natural opiates and work as pain killers and relievers. They diminish and block the perception of pain, inducing and promoting feelings of pleasure and euphoria. They trigger a positive feeling in the body similar to that of morphine but without negative side effects.

Melatonin, which most are familiar with in reference to being a sleep aid, is also an oxytocin booster. It's released in dark, quiet settings, but its production is inhibited or blocked if interrupted or feeling observed. Thinking of this in terms of sleep makes it easy to understand.

As you can readily see, encouraging, supporting, and maximizing the flow of oxytocin should always be the goal in the birth space. Without oxytocin, you have no contractions, and without contractions there's no continual labor progress to get you to the finish line. Not only that, but without high levels of oxytocin you will not *enjoy* the experience the way you are created to. However, it must be reiterated that oxytocin is only released in specific settings, in the context of love. It is not released when you are stressed or fearful!

Fear, stress, and a sense of danger trigger the release of your emergency hormone which is adrenaline. Adrenaline increases your heart and breathing rate for the purpose of making you temporarily faster and stronger, also known as the fight or flight response. Although many mistakenly think adrenaline is what gives them the strength and power to get through birth, the opposite is true. Adrenaline opposes and stops the release and flow of oxytocin! Because emergency hormone actually hinders the birth process, evidently the body does not see birth as an emergency, but rather as a normal, natural, and safe function, just like sleeping or digestion.

When the release of adrenaline does interfere with oxytocin flow, it's very often due to mindsets, beliefs, or external influences contributing to fear or stress, rather than a real physical emergency. That's when, in many instances, synthetic forms of oxytocin like Pitocin® are introduced, citing failure of your body to do its job. In reality, it's usually that the environment your body needed to release the necessary levels of natural oxytocin rather than going into fight or flight mode was not created or facilitated. Your body *can* do its job when properly supported!

Because the part of our brain that controls birth is similar to that of animals, there is benefit in looking at what animals do in labor and birth. Job 12:7a (NLT) says, "Just ask the animals, and they will teach you." Animals trustingly cooperate with the divine design orchestrating their births without over rationalizing or doubting their ability. Most significantly, they understand the importance of their environment. They simply follow their God-given instincts, as many animals prepare a safe, undisturbed, secluded birthing location in a quiet, dark, familiar, and comfortable place. Often it's the same place where they would usually sleep, as though giving birth "at home". When left to themselves, they rarely tear in birth, because they are free to work with the process in whatever way feels and works best. Animals know they need a non threatening atmosphere to give birth easily. They will go into fight or flight mode and can actually regress in labor progress if they feel threatened or fearful. The same is true for humans, although obstetrical education does not acknowledge or teach this fact.

The elephant's birth process is particularly fascinating to observe, as they can become distressed and aggravated if they do not have the support of the other females in their herd, who surround and protect their birth space.

Interestingly, people often tend to have more confidence that birth is going to work well for animals than for humans, and often it does, largely because the animal's birth process is better supported than the human's. Great effort is made to keep laboring animals calm and comfortable by protecting and respecting their space, trying not to interrupt or intrude or do anything that could upset or distress them. They're certainly not going to touch, probe, demand certain positions, or intervene unless absolutely necessary. They know that if they do, the birth process may be delayed or more difficult.

Why not do the same for humans? Why not honor and work with, instead of against, what our bodies physiologically require for an easier and less painful labor and birth?

One of the primary ways we see the physiological design disrupted and even opposed in humans is by over stimulation of the neocortex of the brain. This results in disengagement of the brain stem, thereby inhibiting its ability to efficiently and effectively produce and release the necessary hormonal levels that make things work like they were really meant to. The neocortex is the part of the brain that governs functions such as logic, rationality, thinking, reasoning, analyzing, language, speech, communication, memory, sensory perception, and decision making. Therefore it is stimulated by things like talking, questions that require thought to answer, bright lights, loud or excessive noise, feeling observed or self conscious, or a lack of privacy and intimacy.

Imagine trying to focus on, much less enjoy, reaching climax in sex while being required to engage in conversation requiring deep thought and decision making.

How about if you were being watched, or pressured to finish in a certain amount of time? What if you were repeatedly interrupted, or even just constantly on your guard for possible interruptions? What if you were told not to move too much, or not to make noise? What if things were done to you that you did not want or enjoy? What if what you did want or like was completely disregarded? What if you felt threatened? What if you were scolded like a naive child? What if you're not fully aroused or in the mood? What if you had an earlier argument and there's still tension in the room? What if you're distracted with a lot on your mind? What if you're feeling stressed or worried about something?

Would *any* of these things make it easier to reach sexual climax?

No! In fact, they might even make it *seem* impossible. It's not that you are physically incapable of reaching climax, it's just extremely difficult, perhaps even flat out unattainable, in the wrong settings and conditions. Yet, every scenario I just described is a stimulation of the neocortex and is happening in the birth space on a regular basis! Widely accepted as normal, and often in the name of safety, it actually creates conditions in which no one can feel safe enough to surrender to, much less enjoy, labor and birth. Mothers are led to believe their bodies just don't work, when it's actually the environment and dishonor of their physiological design that doesn't work. Then the cascade of so called necessary interventions begins. It's as preposterous as taking a drug to induce an orgasm deemed unachievable in the presence of an audience telling you what to do, how to do it, and how fast to do it, while poking, prodding, and imposing unnecessary pain and discomfort, topped off with a glaring spotlight on the scene like it's a show.

On the glorious flip side, however, if we can purposefully and intentionally reduce stimulation to the neocortex, we protect and enhance the ability of the brain stem to take over the process, resulting in more ease, less pain, and more pleasure in either sex or birth.

While the brain stem is hardwired and geared to release these essential hormonal concoctions during both birth and sex, as you can probably tell by now, that doesn't mean it always happens automatically or that nothing can interfere with it. There is a very real, strong, mind-body connection, as well as a spiritual one, that can affect this inherent design. The spirit, soul, and body cannot be separated.

The brain is a part of your physical body, but the mind is a part of your soul. As neuroscientist Dr. Caroline Leaf has taught, the mind can literally change the brain![1] Our bodies are originally wired for love (hello oxytocin), but our thinking and choosing either encourage or discourage the ability of our body to function and flourish in its original design. For best outcomes, we must acknowledge the impact of our thinking on our body, and tied in with that, the importance of our surroundings and external influences, since they so greatly affect our thinking.

Now obviously, both sex and birth are still physically possible outside of the physiological model. If that were not so, there would be no such thing as rape or traumatizing birth. Rape, prostitution, and even conception resulting from these actions, are all physically possible even if completely conflicting with the intrinsic blueprint of your brain. Likewise, a harsh, manipulative, fearful, traumatizing, and damaging birth experience still ends with the arrival of a baby.

Just because sexual intercourse, conception, and birth are physically possible under a large variety of circumstances, doesn't mean it was a good or even physiologically normal experience. Likewise, just because it's a common occurrence, that also doesn't make it normal, safe, or good.

My question would be, is any sex or birth outside of our physiological design really safe? That depends largely on how we define safety. If our definition of safety only revolves around what does or does not happen in the physical realm, then in cases such as rape and birth trauma, you would be completely unaffected by the event as soon as it was over, the physical pain stopped, and any physical damage was healed. We all know that's a completely ridiculous notion! We know that what happens on the inside, in your soul, is actually a way bigger deal than what happens on the outside. It's what you carry with you most. It is truthfully said that a woman never forgets how she felt or was made to feel during birth, whether positive or negative. Physical pain does exacerbate anything bad that's happening to you, but it's also possible to experience physical pain without being traumatized, which indicates that the greater issue is a non physical one. I could accidentally stub my toe, burn my finger, or even break a bone without carrying fear and trauma the rest of my life because of it. Now, if it was done to me *on purpose*, that could change how I feel, think of, and remember it.

To call either birth or sex safe we must take into account how it affects the person as a whole, not just physically. Whether or not there is physical pain, damage, or consequence is not the only gauge. You can't tell women that, "healthy mom, healthy baby is what matters", if all that means is that they're alive and not permanently physically damaged. If they arrive on the other side wounded in any way - physically, emotionally, mentally, or spiritually - then that was not a truly safe or healthy experience. Likewise, if a "safe" label on sex requires nothing more than consent and protection against pregnancy or disease, but does not take into account whether there is any detriment or ramification apart from the physical, it cannot be called truly safe. Every time you experience sex or birth, whether inside or outside of God's plan for you, it affects you as a whole person and not just your physical body.

What then truly does make sex and birth good and safe, physically, emotionally, mentally, and spiritually?

Truly safe sex only happens when a man and woman mutually, freely, and fully give all of themselves to each other. Not just their bodies, but their hearts, their commitment, their futures, their faithfulness, and their vulnerability. For safe sex to take place you must be able to let go of all inhibitions, wholeheartedly and without distraction giving yourself to the event. In the same way, safe birth is also about being able to let go of all inhibitions in order to fully surrender to the journey. This art of letting go, either in sex or birth, is virtually impossible when you're in the wrong environment with the wrong people, or simply have a deep, inner knowing that something about the situation is just not right. Truly safe sex and birth can only happen when the heart feels, and is, safe.

If you can't look back on it without some kind of regret, shame, disgust, or sadness, it probably wasn't safe sex.

If you are left with a sense of loss, emptiness, or something missing, it probably wasn't safe sex.

If when it's over you once again feel unsatisfied, even if you had brief pleasure in the moment, it probably wasn't within the protective boundaries of truly safe sex.

Safe sex won't leave you disturbed, ashamed, or harmed in any way, whether physically, emotionally, mentally, or spiritually. Please understand this isn't meant to imply that every time you have sex it has to be an earth shattering experience of mind boggling ecstasy in order to be deemed good or safe. There is a vast difference between sex that produces pain or negative feelings and sex that just wasn't super glorious simply because you were tired or had a lot on your mind.

If we don't understand the importance of, or have any frame of reference for healthy, safe sex, it becomes that much more difficult to connect the dots between good sex and good birth. If our view and experience of sex has been perverted or twisted, it will probably also be more challenging to see birth for what it really is - beautiful and safe.

However, if we experience sex as God designed it to be, and apply what we know makes sex good to the birth space, it will be so much easier to also experience birth as God intended.

Before I close this chapter, I want to make sure you know that even if you've never had that good, safe sex and yet have conceived, you can still give birth differently than you conceived, inside the safety and pleasure of God's perfect design!

6 the need for intimacy

Everything discussed in the previous chapter can be largely summed up as a need for intimacy. An environment of intimacy agrees and works in harmony with the physiological design of our body. Intimacy is also what takes you where you need to be mentally, emotionally, and spiritually for sex and birth to be enjoyable and safe. Intimacy is not just a physical act, nor is it relevant only in sexual context. It's also a state of mind and condition of the heart. The fact that we, as women, are such suckers for romance proves this! I mean, c'mon. We all know that the best sex doesn't start in the bedroom. It starts with largely non physical things, like his romancing of you, which he can only do well by really knowing you and what is meaningful to you personally. That's a huge part of the intimacy that leads to great sex.

Sex should be the fruit of intimacy, an expression of inner intimacy that has already occurred beforehand between two people. If sex is the sole and entire extent of your understanding of intimacy, you've merely scratched the surface. Inner intimacy has to do with knowing and being known. A deep knowing and understanding between two people is what makes their sex genuinely meaningful. Interestingly, the King James Bible translates accounts of sex as, "He *knew* his wife."

Our deeply rooted need for intimacy is actually a desire to be fully known and fully loved for who we really are, which is one of the most pleasurable, deeply satisfying things in this life. There are some places in you that can never be touched or visited without intimacy. This is why Eden was a place of pleasure, because God and man had true intimacy, with nothing causing separation between them. Psalm 139 and the entire book of Song of Solomon paint a breathtaking picture of what it is like to be known and loved in this way.

Intimacy's pleasure goes far beyond a brief moment of physical gratification only. It will pleasure you through and through - spirit, soul, and body - leaving you satisfied to your core, yet always longing for more.

There is no intimacy as deep and great as that with Jesus, because only He knows you completely, inside and out. However, even intimacy with Jesus doesn't just happen automatically. The garden of intimacy must be kept, guarded, and cultivated. Often laziness is to blame for a lack of intimacy, because cultivating that garden is work.

Intimacy is a result of growing some roots in a relationship. How do roots grow down deep? With time. By being watered, fed, nourished, cared for, and protected. This doesn't happen in a one night stand, between friends with benefits, through casual sex, rape or prostitution.

None of those sexual encounters meet your physiological and spiritual need for intimacy in every sense of the word.

Intimacy requires an intimate, private setting. Three really can be a crowd. Sometimes you have to shut the door and be alone. Intimate things shared with everyone are no longer intimate. The things most precious are those that take place in the context of intimacy, but putting everything out there for everyone to see and know causes the precious to become common. Intimacy becomes foreign and rare.

This is one reason why I've never really been able to jump on the bandwagon of being transparent and vulnerable with all the world, although for many that seems to have become the measuring stick to judge how "real" someone is. While I understand that there is a time, place, and degree to which we need to be those things with people, not everything you carry is for everybody.

There are intimate things that are just between you and Jesus, just between you and your spouse, just for you and your family, or just between you and that one friend. I've seen too many opportunities for intimacy in the birth space stolen due to ignorance, pressure, or a feeling of obligation to people who assume they are entitled to be involved, but are actually disturbing the need for intimacy. You don't have to take everyone along for the ride. Those whom you give access to your intimate birth space should understand that with it comes the responsibility to do everything in their power to respect and protect that intimacy.

Intimacy demands trust and is impossible without it. It requires safety and a sense of security. You cannot open up to or *willingly* lay yourself bare before someone without trusting that it's safe to do so.

Intimacy cannot happen without vulnerability. In fact, intimacy creates vulnerability, because I can't be intimate with you without vulnerability. However, becoming vulnerable outside of intimacy and opening up to someone who has not mutually done so results in getting hurt. Birth is one of the most vulnerable times in life, and because so often that place of vulnerability is taken advantage of, so many become traumatized.

Right on the other hand, vulnerability within the protection of intimacy results in one of the most profound, euphoric experiences of your life. It creates bonds with those you share it with like nothing else can. Because of the vulnerable nature of both birth and sex, they could be either some of the worst, most traumatizing things you ever experience, or, in the context of love and intimacy, some of the best, most fulfilling gifts from God you get to enjoy in this life.

Real intimacy doesn't exist outside of love. When love is king, you won't feel used, abused, or taken advantage of. It's the difference between feeling like something happened to you versus feeling like you were a willing and eager participant. Intimacy will respect you.

Obviously you can always just go through the physical motions, but outside of the environment of intimacy neither birth nor sex will reach the peak of their potential for pleasure or ease of function. For maximum intimacy to be attained, you must be fully present, welcoming and anticipating the event. Your heart must be wide open and your mind fully yielded. You must minimize and eliminate distractions and interruptions. You must intentionally release any restraint in spirit, soul, or body. When the conditions for intimacy are met, the physical body will respond accordingly. In the context of sex, this is when it's easiest to become sexually aroused. The more aroused you are the easier, quicker, and more pleasurable it is to reach climax. Birth works exactly the same way! Your brain and body will respond to the environment of intimacy, because it's what they are wired to do! Your body will open more easily, more quickly, with less pain, and with more pleasure.

This kind of need for intimacy is why giving birth at home or in a homelike environment can have such a hugely positive impact on the birth process. Some definitions of the word home include: a familiar setting, a congenial environment, and the focus of one's domestic attention. Home really is where the heart is, and the heart must be deeply involved to achieve intimacy. Not only that, but your home is where you have the most authority and ability to set the atmosphere and control the environment. There really is no place like home, and nothing does for you what "home" does.

Home is not necessarily always about a physical location, but also about a presence or condition of the heart. It might be less about where everyone is acquainted and familiarities abound, and more about where you can be who you are and where you're fully known and loved. Home is where there is trust and love. Ephesians 3:17 (NLT), "Christ will make His home in your hearts as you trust in Him. Your roots will grow down into God's love and keep you strong."

We must ask, what is home to me? When, where, and with whom do I feel most "at home"? These answers will help you see where it would be easiest to create and maintain an environment of intimacy, and with whom you do or do not want to share that space.

We must also remember intimacy can only happen as an act of the will of all parties involved. If it's not mutual, it's not intimacy. It's not one always consenting and the other always making demands.

Intimacy cannot be forced. That's not intimacy at all, but rather abuse. Jesus never forces you into anything. He always waits for your yes.

The reason that our faith pleases God is that it opens the door of access for Him to come in and do what He longs to do, which is to give us pleasure, and make our world like Eden. Psalm 36:8 (TPT), "All may drink of the anointing from the abundance of your house. All may drink their fill from the delightful springs of Eden." For Him to be able to give me that pleasure I must open the door with my faith. He will never force His way in, even to give me something good, because being forced is never pleasurable.

Jesus has set the greatest example by taking the initiative, the first step toward intimacy with you, in that He first gave Himself before asking you to give yourself. This is how you know you can safely yield to Him. He never asks you to make yourself vulnerable without first having made Himself vulnerable. He'd never ask you to trust Him with your body without first having given His. He's not in it just to get something from you, but to give something to you. He'll never wrongly take advantage of you. He'll never violate your will. He'll never leave you disappointed because intimacy with Him always satisfies.

Ephesians 5:29 (TPT), "No one abuses his own body, but pampers it — serving and satisfying its needs. That's exactly what Christ does for his church! He serves and satisfies us as members of his body." The AMP translation says He nourishes, protects, and cherishes His body. It then goes on to say, '"A man leaves his father and mother and is joined to his wife, and the two are united into one.' This is a great mystery, but it is an illustration of the way Christ and the church are one." (NLT) Notice Jesus doesn't serve His own convenience above yours. He left His Father and His home, the glory and perfection of Heaven, so He could become one with you. Oneness equals intimacy.

That's the kind of treatment He desires for a laboring woman, that she be saturated with His love for His bride. As we've seen, even our anatomy and physiology agree with this. That love is what enables her to yield herself to intimacy and pleasure, deepening and intensifying the powerful bonds of oneness. God gave us as mothers this exclusive gift of opportunity for an unmatched, unrivaled encounter with Him. Many women have testified that they have never felt closer to God or sensed the anointing so strongly as in birth. The anointing makes things personal and intimate.

Yet, how many women have been robbed of this experience because their will was violated, their vulnerability abused, and their need for intimacy disregarded, being expected to bend and conform to the convenience of another while those demanding such made no similar effort? How many are served and satisfied as Jesus does for His bride, making it easy to yield to His perfect design, in power and strength?

Such questions are not meant to fuel either a victim or entitlement mentality, but to encourage you to look to Jesus as your source! When He's your source, He is the one you go to for guidance on every decision you need to make surrounding your birth. He leads you into the right choices for you, your baby, and family. He won't lead you into pain and disappointment. However, you must willingly and intentionally give Him every decision, every desire, every care, and every fear, because He'll never just force you into what's right or best.

You can't have a profoundly intimate birth experience by standing aloof from it. It will require you to plunge new depths and scale new heights. It takes faith and courage to open yourself up to that level. Sometimes the thought of it may scare us, perhaps because our vulnerability has been abused in the past. Oh, but the reward, when by faith you trust Jesus with your heart and experience a new level of intimacy!

As you develop this intimacy with Him, which means really getting to know Him, His heart, and His character, then He'll be able to show you what to do and how to do it in order to create and maintain an Eden-like birth environment. You will hear an anointed Word from Him that is specific, personal, and tailor made to you and your situation. When you act on that word, the outcome will be pleasurable and satisfying!

7 choice

If God has redeemed us from the curse of sorrowful childbirth, has delivered us from fear, wants us to have a satisfying birth experience, and has physiologically designed us to give birth peacefully and without complication, then why are so many births still the opposite of that? How are disappointment, fear, and sorrow still finding a way in? Why, especially among believers, are there not more women experiencing Eden-like birth?

When an outcome doesn't agree with what is revealed as God's will for us in His Word, we must have the courage to ask Him for His wisdom and revelation-knowledge as to why. Without getting honest answers to challenging questions like these, the faith of someone who believes and prays for something that doesn't pan out can be hurt, or worse, they may conclude that faith doesn't even work. Yet, the truth is, God has always intended that there be power, which is the ability to get results, in our faith and prayers.

Sometimes, the real answers to these questions are hard to swallow, but that's still better than going with the mainstream response of automatically questioning God's good will toward you. It's comforting to know that you know the truth, even if the truth is not always comfortable.

That which keeps women from experiencing birth as God intended is not a matter of God not keeping His Word or not wanting you to have that experience. He's not looking for reasons to withhold His goodness from you. "He who did not spare His own Son, but delivered Him over for us all, how will He not also with Him freely give us all things?" (Romans 8:32 NASB)

God never fails. His Word is unchanging, forever settled in Heaven. He's not of a double minded nature who cannot be trusted to mean what He says.

So if God's not the problem, what is?

While every situation is unique, and there are some answers that can only be revealed to you directly by the Lord, generally speaking, I've observed some key factors that often play a role in undesirable labor and birth experiences.

One significant thing I see negatively affect birth experiences, especially among Christians, is confusion about God's will and sovereignty. The belief that whatever God wants will happen, or that nothing happens without His permission, is inseparably linked to a major underestimation of the power and responsibility of our God-given freedom of choice.

Our choices impact outcomes as much or more than God's will. However, the more strongly you believe that God is in control of everything, the more lightly you will take your privilege and responsibility to make wise choices.

Why did God tell the people of Israel to make a choice in Joshua 24:15? If He is in complete control of all, what difference would their choice have made?

Religion has cleverly shifted the responsibility for every outcome onto the sovereignty of God, disregarding that in His sovereignty, He gave us a free will, with power and authority to choose, which He will never override or violate. The idea that the reason why something prayed for doesn't happen is because it's not God's will is readily accepted simply because it's the most comfortable and convenient to the flesh. When you don't have answers, or you don't want to know the truth about what happened, or you don't want to invest in seeking the truth, it's easiest just to say that God is in control. Not only does that excuse you from learning to know God's will, you also don't have to acknowledge the fact that maybe it had something to do with your choices. It provides justification for remaining ignorant, sometimes even willfully, and absolving yourself of any responsibility.

The flesh doesn't like the work of tending the garden.

Thinking that everything is up to God also hinders you from developing decisiveness about what you want, crippling your ability to make good decisions. If you don't know what you want, there's a big chance you'll get something you don't want. A passive attitude that just goes with the flow of others' desires will usually take you some place you don't want to be. Some people are so sovereignty-of-God minded that they don't even give thought to what they want. Yet, as Philippians 2:13 says, there are desires that God Himself puts in you. Those desires are not selfish, but rather are meant to serve as a compass, helping you make quality choices and decisions, which is vitally important in something like birth.

If people actually believed the scriptures that say we will receive whatever we ask and believe for in prayer, they would be a lot more attentive to both seeking God's will and considering the desires of their heart, because that would enable them to pray according to His will. They could then pray with confidence and in true faith. Instead, assuming His will is revealed by whether or not He answers their prayer, they casually throw up some prayers, hoping something will stick, but not actually believing there's ever any guarantee that He'll do anything they ask. They think He's just going to do whatever He sees fit. If indeed we are not involved in determining whether God's will is done in our life, then why is the Bible full of scriptures telling us to pray, ask, know the will of God, and have faith in God?

It's by His design that we actively participate in the fulfillment of His will and plan for our lives. If it were not so, our heart would not be engaged. If the extent of our involvement was simply praying, "just do whatever You think is best", it wouldn't require any real intimacy with Him or substantial investment into the relationship on our end. God is always after your heart.

The good news is, there *is* a way to ask God for something and actually get it, as laid out for us in I John 5:14-15 (AMP):

"This is the [remarkable degree of] confidence which we [as believers are entitled to] have before Him: that if we ask anything according to His will, [that is, consistent with His plan and purpose] He hears us. And if we know [for a fact, as indeed we do] that He hears and listens to us in whatever we ask, we [also] know [with settled and absolute knowledge] that we have [granted to us] the requests which we have asked from Him."

As you can see, the first thing that has to happen is knowing His will. That's where faith begins! If you're not fully convinced that something is God's will for you - if you leave room for doubt or exceptions - you cannot fully believe in your heart that it will be done for you. Prayer then becomes nothing more than a groundless wish presented to God, without any assurance that it will be heard or granted. On the contrary, when your request is based on the will of God found in the Word of God, there is great power in your prayer. It takes out the guesswork and you can confidently expect what you ask for!

Now, you're completely free to decide that you're not going to make such a big deal of seeking God's plan for your pregnancy and birth, rather just trusting that whatever God wants is what will happen. In His mercy and grace, He'll still meet you where you are and do everything

He can to help you, just like He did for me before I realized I needed to take more responsibility in tending and keeping the garden. However, neither you nor I can then blame Him for a less than satisfying outcome if we are the ones who fail to ask, seek, and knock. If our own choices create an entirely different scenario than we are praying for, it's not God's fault.

As we find in James 2:17, faith must be accompanied by actions and choices that align and correspond with what you say you're believing for. In speaking of Abraham's faith, James 2:22 (TPT) says, "Can't you see how his action cooperated with his faith and by his action faith found its full expression?"

Let's say you are believing for a completely fear free pregnancy and birth. You then choose to hire a care provider whose entire practice is founded on a pathological view of birth. That means they are expectantly looking for problems that would require their intervention. They are constantly feeding you fear based, what-if information, and you have to fight fiercely every step of the way to remain unwaveringly peaceful in the face of every negative, daunting thing you're being told. Come labor and delivery, once again you purposely place yourself into a system whose core policies and routine practices are based on the fear of risks, as though you must be rescued from the very thing you are believing to have no fear about.

Is it going to be easy to remain fear free in that type of environment surrounded with that type of conversation? No! While it's true that we do not have to allow outward circumstances to dictate our inner peace, being subjected to a long hard fight from the beginning of pregnancy all the way to birth will too often simply wear you down to the point that fear manages to creep in to some degree. Then, when the fear free experience which you were believing for is not realized, you may feel defeated, angry, or at the very least, disappointed. You may even question why God allowed it or didn't help you more. Yet, could it be that choices you made all along the way were influencing factors that gave place to fear? Did your choices truly agree with your goals and what you prayed for?

When evaluating our choices and their impact, we must ask questions like, "Am I choosing a care provider who feeds me fear? Am I choosing a birthing location that wouldn't allow me to follow the lead of my body as designed by God? Am I choosing the diet and lifestyle that lead to the complication that requires undesired intervention? Am I choosing to allow voices of fear to speak into my life, whether through friends, family, birth workers, or Google® ?"

As another example, you may fully believe that it's God's will for you to have a healthy, strong pregnancy, but does eating junk food in front of the TV for hours on end align, agree, and correspond with your faith for wholeness in your body?

Can we purposely, without hearing from God to do so, put ourselves in situations that create a high risk of producing something other than what we say we're believing for, and call that "walking by faith"? Is there true agreement in that?

While we clearly have a responsibility to make wise choices that create a welcoming environment for what we are believing to see, sadly, there are many instances in birth where that freedom of choice is wrongfully stripped from women. To be violated by having things done to them or their baby against their will is never, ever ok.

However, perhaps if we more closely contemplated the choices made leading up to that type of scenario we could much more often avoid it. Please understand my heart in this. This is not about blaming the victim or perpetuating guilt and condemnation. It's never about shifting the moral responsibility of a care provider or maternal care system onto the mother. There is absolutely no excuse for introducing trauma when it was in their power to do otherwise. What this is about, is helping you understand how to do everything in your God given power to prevent finding yourself in a traumatizing, violating, or even just disappointing situation to begin with. That is largely done by making wise choices that agree with what you want and pray for.

Even when your freedom of choice has not been taken from you, the devil likes to apply pressure until you *feel* like you don't have a choice, at least not a good one. In John 8:3-11, when the religious leaders brought a woman caught in adultery to Jesus, it looked like He only had two bad options. Either He could agree to stoning her as was written in their law, or He could become a lawbreaker, giving them grounds to accuse Him. Instead, He listened for the voice of His Father to give Him option C. When you feel stuck between a rock and a hard place, God has an option C! It's a choice you couldn't think up on your own and the devil never sees it coming.

I say this with all the love in my heart. The fact is that sometimes women simply don't want the responsibility of choice or the responsibility of tending the garden. In the area of healthy food choices for example, some have told me directly they just don't like to do the work of research, basically inferring that I should do it for them. While I love to help people, taking on their responsibility as my own is not ultimately helping them.

It may be tempting to think that if you just do what your doctor, or mother, or doula tells you rather than making educated choices for yourself, then it's not your fault if something doesn't go right, making it easy to blame someone else. But, did you know that anyone who is willing to make your choices for you, telling you exactly what to do, is usually not equally willing to take responsibility for the outcome? They may be quick to take away your freedom of choice, but instead of admitting fault for any negative ramifications that occur as a result of what they pushed for, they'll shift the blame back on you, citing what you should have done differently, even when you were following their bidding to begin with. This goes for anyone, whether a doctor, hospital, midwife, doula, mother, grandparent, or friend. Those who want to control your decisions will not typically accept liability for undesirable end results.

Ultimately you will be the one held accountable for outcomes, which is why it's so important that you make your own prayerfully researched and fully informed choices. You need to have the peace of knowing you made the best possible choices for you and your baby.

This doesn't mean you can't ask anyone for help in making those decisions, but you do so with the understanding that ultimately, *you* are the one who must take responsibility for following the advice given.

While we as birth workers can definitely offer wisdom and insight based on our own research and things we've personally seen and experienced, we have to be mindful of not saying things like "you should" or "I would" too much. If we excessively push our own preferences we can cross the line of helping you get the information you need to make your choice over to finding ourselves trying to control your decisions. Sometimes it's a fine line, but nevertheless, it's a line we need to honor and be keenly aware of.

A controlling spirit is in direct opposition to the nature of God, because it doesn't want you to have a choice. God leads; He doesn't push. He says "follow Me", but doesn't prod or drag us. He stands at the door and knocks instead of just forcing His way in (Revelation 3:20). He is the least controlling person you will ever meet!

In fact, God is 100% pro-choice. Being pro-choice is an attribute of God that has been distorted by the devil to be understood to mean being pro-abortion. However, to be truly pro-choice is as far removed from being pro-abortion as the true symbolism of a rainbow is from gay pride. If you are truly pro-choice, you want every person to have a choice, including the unborn. However, abortion is all about taking away the choice of a human being who is in a position where they cannot speak for themselves, making it that much more egregious.

Freedom of choice originates with God, coming out of His very nature. It's an inherent right we have because God decided to give it to us. It is not a selfish, rebellious, or fleshly demand we came up with on our own. God created us to be thinking, choosing individuals with a free will. The very evidence of this is that we feel violated when others make choices for us that should have been ours to make. It's why we feel despair even when it *seems* like we don't have a choice, whether or not that's actually true. It's why we must be healed from the trauma that can occur when things are done to us or we are forced into something against our will. It's why everyone resents being pressured or forced.

One of the greatest proofs of God's love is that He always gives us a choice. He knows our heart could never be in something that's forced on us, and the heart is what He's most interested in. He is so adamant about protecting the free will He gave us that He's even willing to take the risk of allowing us to make bad choices that will harm us. He loves freedom so much that He even gives us the freedom to say no to the very things that would be best for us.

Using force, making someone feel there's no way out, or that the only choice they have is a bad one, is the devil's way. Anything that is forced does not originate with the Spirit of God, because where His Spirit is, there is freedom. (II Corinthians 3:17) Unless you have a choice, you're not really free.

The worst kind of abuser is the one who says they're doing it because they love you. Yet this is what millions believe about God, that He would violate their will and purposely cause them pain in the name of love. God is not an abusive Father, and Jesus is not an abusive husband.

Now, we must understand that just because we have the freedom to choose, not every choice will be free of grave repercussions. Even rapists, pimps, murderers, traffickers, and slave owners have the free will to make those evil choices, but because their choices violate and strip another person of the right to choose, there must be laws implemented for protection of freedom. Being pro-choice is not a license for evil or about promoting a lifestyle where you can do whatever you want, whenever you want, however you want, with, or to, whomever you want.

In birth, or anything else, it's important to understand that there's also a big difference between consenting to something and voluntarily choosing something. In order to make a real choice, you must have options. You must know what those options are, along with their risks and benefits. This is called informed choice.

Being asked for consent is good, while informed consent is even better. However, neither are the same as informed choice.

To illustrate, here are some examples of all three:

Asking for consent is a simple request for permission without any mention of risks, benefits, or alternative options. Example: "Is it okay if I check your cervix?"

Informed consent is a request for permission along with information on the risks and benefits of the proposed action, but without discussion of alternative options. Example: "I would like to break your water. This is how we do that (explains procedure). One of the possible risks is an increased risk of infection. We will also want you to give birth by a certain time after your water is broken and it may make contractions more intense. The possible benefit is that it may speed up labor. May I go ahead and break it?"

Informed choice involves a detailed conversation surrounding all your possible options, their risks and benefits, and your freedom to make the choice that you are most comfortable with. Example: "Let's talk about induction. We could attempt natural, more gentle means like herbs, nipple stimulation, intercourse, chiropractic care, acupuncture, or optimal positioning techniques. We could also do a membrane sweep, break your water, or use a foley bulb. Prostaglandins and Pitocin ® are options for medical induction. Simply waiting for spontaneous labor is also an option. Here are the risks and benefits of all these choices so that you can best decide what you would like to do. (lists risks and benefits)."

Telling you what they are going to do without asking your permission, or worse, doing whatever they want without even telling you what that is, does not fall into any of the above categories. Saying, "we're just going to check how far along you are", is not asking for consent. Pretending your water just so happened to break while they checked your cervix when they actually did it on purpose without asking or telling you, is a complete violation of your right to choose.

Not only is God the master example of always giving people a choice, He's also the Master of informed choice. He tells us exactly what will happen if we make the right choice, and exactly what will happen if we make the wrong one. He'll never withhold information you would need to make a truly informed choice in an effort to sway you in a certain direction. He will draw you with His love and kindness toward the best choice, but like a gentleman, He'll still let you do the choosing.

Once we believe and accept the responsibility we've been given through freedom of choice, and realize the extensive impact of our choices, we will pay much closer attention to what and how we choose. We will thoughtfully weigh the pros and cons, risks and benefits, viewing every choice as a seed that will produce a harvest, either good or bad. We will wisely count the cost. We will diligently seek the truth, not only facts, to guide our decisions. When our choices agree with His will and plan for us, becoming the corresponding action to our confession of faith, that's when things work the way both He and we desire!

8 choosing a birth team

I believe that one of the greatest decisions to impact your birth is your choice of care provider and birth team, including any family or friends you choose to have present at your birth. While the right and responsibility of choice as it pertains to your birth belongs to you, you must understand that when you hire a provider you are giving a degree of authority or jurisdiction over what happens at your birth to them as well. Anyone given that kind of access should be someone you can walk in wholehearted agreement with.

The process of choosing a provider typically looks like a search for someone you feel is well qualified and experienced who also takes your insurance and/or is affordable. Some take it a step farther by inquiring whether the provider's routine practices agree with the type of birth they envision, like limiting intervention perhaps. The majority of maternity care relationships in this country are usually pretty formal. Interaction between provider and client is brief and impersonal, often feeling like you're just a number. There's not a whole lot of time or opportunity to build rapport and when you arrive at birth, they still seem pretty much like a stranger.

There's not necessarily anything inherently wrong with any of the above. Obviously, we have to be able to afford the person we hire. Obviously, we all want a wise, intelligent provider who is fully competent to handle anything that may arise with clarity of mind and dependable skill. Perhaps becoming chummy friends doesn't take precedence over the importance of their job qualifications. However, what is it that really makes someone wise and reliable in their line of work? Is it only their degree of training and education, level of experience, or the number of stars in their reviews? What if there's more to determining which provider is best for you?

James 3:13-15 helps us clearly distinguish between earthly, natural wisdom and the wisdom that comes from Heaven by spelling out for us the fruits of each.

"Who among you is wise and intelligent? Let him by his good conduct show his [good] deeds with the gentleness and humility of true wisdom. But if you have bitter jealousy and selfish ambition in your hearts, do not be arrogant, and [as a result] be in defiance of the truth. This [superficial] wisdom is not that which comes down from above, but is earthly [secular], natural [unspiritual], even demonic." (AMP)

The so called wisdom of the world is marked by jealousy, contention, rivalry, and selfish ambition. All of these are tightly intertwined and rooted in pride, which is actually a face of fear. It goes on to tell us in verse 16 what the end result of these hallmarks will be. "For where jealousy and selfish ambition exist, there is disorder [unrest, rebellion] and every evil thing and morally degrading practice." Some translations of this verse also use words like confusion, disharmony, many troubles, and meanness. What the world calls wisdom is simply being sharp witted and clever enough to get to the top of the proverbial ladder, regardless of how you do it and who you hurt along the way. We must keep in mind what the ultimate harvest of that kind of earthly, selfish wisdom will always be. If you don't want confusion, disunity, unrest, trouble, and meanness showing up at your birth, you cannot invite people in who are constantly sowing selfish seeds of jealousy, strife and competition.

Verse 17 of James 3 further describes the characteristics of God's wisdom, revealing that those who walk in it have no hidden agenda, ulterior motives, or deceitfulness in their heart, making room for true unity. "But the wisdom from above is first pure [morally and spiritually undefiled], then peace-loving [courteous, considerate], gentle, reasonable [and willing to listen], full of compassion and good fruits. It is unwavering, without [self-righteous] hypocrisy [and self-serving guile]." Someone walking in that kind of heavenly wisdom is the truly intelligent person you want on your team!

II Corinthians 1:12 (TPT) reiterates this. "God has empowered us to conduct ourselves in a holy manner and with no hidden agenda. God's marvelous grace enables us to minister to everyone with pure motives, not in the clever wisdom of the world."

According to James 3:13, true wisdom produces a humility. Therefore, to identify a provider or anyone else who is wise and intelligent beyond the superficial level of degrees, titles, and social status, the first thing you do is look for humility. The more real, Godly wisdom they walk in, the more humble they will be. I Corinthians 8:2 (NLT) says, "Anyone who claims to know all the answers doesn't really know very much." That reminds me of the old saying, "The more you know, the more you realize how much you don't know." An intelligent person won't get all puffed up with knowledge, position, or power. They understand that the fear of the Lord is the beginning of wisdom (Proverbs 9:10), and without it, the initials after their name don't really mean a thing. Because they fear the Lord, they also hate pride (Proverbs 8:13), which in contrast, always accompanies the world's wisdom. They understand that pride limits the grace they need to do their job at the highest level of excellence possible. James 4:6b (TPT), "God resists you when you are proud but continually pours out grace when you are humble."

Humility will produce kindness, while pride is a precursor of rudeness.

When humility walks out, rudeness walks in.

Prideful, self centered people will degrade others to make themselves look or feel better. If their position or so called authority is ever questioned or challenged they'll often respond in anger or frustration, or by belittling and shaming the offender. They can't walk away from strife and arguing for fear that it might look like they are actually yielding to someone else, which they are never willing to do. They won't admit when they're wrong or that there's a better way if they can't take the credit for it.

A prideful care provider doesn't want to give you options because that creates opportunity for you to choose. They don't think you really need to have a choice, because how could you possibly know better than they anyway? In the case they suspect that you're leaning toward a choice they don't like, they will often start to list all the risks of said option in an attempt to persuade you otherwise, while never mentioning the risks of the choice *they* want you to make.

While it makes them feel superior, like they have the upper hand, ultimately pride will always make them prey. It's a dangerous road that always leads to a fall. (Proverbs 16:18; 18:12)

Prideful people also tend to be very controlling. They're afraid if they don't maintain control they will be unsuccessful, overlooked, and dismissed, their dreams and desires never realized. Because they look to themselves as their source rather than God, they'll do whatever they think they have to for self preservation or promotion, whether that's using fear tactics, deception, or threats. They believe their path to success and increase is found in their ability to manipulate or force others to do what will benefit themselves.

When someone sees themselves as their own source, they'll often want *you* to see them as *your* source too. They want you to have to depend on them for every decision, because that way they can maintain control. By telling you exactly what you can or cannot do at all times, they act as though your success is contingent on whether or not you follow their orders. This God-complex is an attempt at domination over others. God gave us dominion over the earth, not over each other. He intended for us to be free of human domination so we could be at liberty to depend on Him alone as our Source. If we truly love someone we will not try to make ourselves their source, nor allow *them* to make us their source, because that limits them to only what we can do or be for them. If we want them to learn to fully trust in God as their Source, we've got to stop trying to assume the role of the Holy Spirit in their decision making.

Those who do make God their source will have no problem with you doing the same. They won't take offense if you give Him that place rather than them. They won't get mad if instead of immediately agreeing with their suggestions or advice, you say you first need to hear from the Lord about it. When God is their Source, they won't act competitive and territorial or show prejudice and favoritism.

How do you recognize a controlling spirit? Look at what the response is when it doesn't get its way. Does it bring shame, blame, condemnation, fear, offense or rejection? Does it create fear of those things?

It's hard to forget holding a distressed mother's hand, working to keep eye contact with her so she will tune into my voice rather than that of the arrogant doctor who is becoming stern with her. Even a simple explanation of what he was doing inside of her could have served to calm and reassure her, but instead he thought speaking to her like a child would be more helpful. The same doctor, during the delivery of

114

the placenta, decided he needed to randomly air his opinion on why people shouldn't give birth outside of hospitals due to the risk of hemorrhage. As a doula who also attended out of hospital births, his comment was obviously directed toward me, and was completely irrelevant to this particular birth. The only thing his territorial remark served to accomplish was to give mom another unnecessary scare. She understood him to be saying *she* was the one hemorrhaging! You see, when your mind is on yourself, your position, and your reputation you will say and do stupid things that hurt the people around you, even if you yourself are completely oblivious to it. You cannot have your eyes on yourself while simultaneously looking out for mother's and baby's best interests.

It may or may not come as a surprise to you, but pride, competition, and a controlling spirit are probably the greatest downfalls of birth workers all across the board, from midwives to doulas, to doctors and nurses. I've seen it in the younger, who let their position of prominence go to their head, and I've seen it in the older, who are so set in their ways they won't change a thing despite what evidence says to the contrary about what would be better for mom and baby.

These negative characteristics in birth workers can often be spotted more easily in the way they speak of and interact with others in their field of work than in their dealings with clients. Believe it or not, you can have super skilled birth workers who are wonderfully kind and loving to their clients, but mean as a hornet to other birth workers whom they perceive to be a threat or competition. Unfortunately, much too frequently they feel the need to defend themselves and their territory.

Listen closely to how the doctor talks about midwives. Listen closely to how the midwife talks about doctors. Listen closely to how the doula talks about other doulas. It will tell you a lot about whether they're walking in the world's wisdom or God's wisdom!

Sadly, even many who are believers still largely operate in the world's wisdom rather than God's when it comes to their job. They act like the work place is an area of life that's exempt of the need to implement Godly wisdom and principles because "it's just business". In fact, they often see it as impractical. After all, how are you going to make the highest potential income if you don't push for interventions that put more money in your pocket? How will you get your quota in for the month if you spend more time with your clients, actually listening to their concerns, questions, and dreams? What will happen to your job if you refuse to cooperate with policies that put mother and baby at greater risk? Keep in mind, this isn't about salvation status, but about the inner motives and priorities directing what they are willing to do to maintain status quo or advance in their field.

Is the law of love governing the way they treat people both inside and outside of business, or do they have double standards? Is it enough if they walk in love *only* toward their clients?

Do they closely attend to staying at the top of their game by continuing education and serving their clients with excellence, but simultaneously resent others in their field of work, treating and speaking of them wrongly to try and get ahead or maintain their illusion of authority and rank?

Under the guise of making decisions that are "best for business", do they purposely defraud others and try to bring them to ruin? Since when is that ok just because "it's business"?

Does the law of sowing and reaping not apply in this arena? To be clear, I've seen these types of actions among both doctors *and* midwives, as well as all other types of birth workers such as doulas, etc.

You may think, "Jackie, you're making a mountain out of a molehill! My provider's possible issues with someone else have nothing to do with me or my birth." You see, it's easy for the client also to have an "it's just business" attitude. "C'mon! I'm just looking for a care provider, not a marriage partner!" No, we're not looking for a flawless human, but spiritual laws do come into play here. Just because it's not you personally they have a problem with, doesn't mean the harvest of their bitter rivalry with someone else will not splash over into your world if you have invited them into it. We have to put two and two together. The envy in their heart toward someone else can result in confusion and trouble at your birth, because unless they've repented, you cannot separate a person's harvest from that person.

"So what am I supposed to do? Dig up every bit of dirt I can find on someone before hiring them? Interrogate them about every one of their relationships to make sure they don't hold anything against anyone?"

Again, no. This is why we need the Holy Spirit! As you tune in to His voice and gaze into His perfection, He is the one who shows you when something is off, helping you pick up on impure motives springing from pride and selfishness, resulting in a territorial spirit.

What are some examples of what could happen if you have a provider or birth worker who allows their distorted desire to prove a point become a greater influence in their practice than the best interests of mom and baby? You could have a doctor who, because of an urge to flex his hierarchical muscle, makes a poor call for an unnecessary c-section. You could have a midwife who ignores the signs of a need for transfer because they feel they must prove that home birth always works. You could have a doula who steps out of her scope of practice because they want to prove a medical care provider is unnecessary. Perhaps the midwife or doula resents doctors and hospitals, or the doctors and hospitals hate the midwife or doula. This can drive any one of them to do irresponsible things.

A mama I know personally went to the hospital after her home birth due to a retained placenta. She was not too proud or so desperate to prove a point that she refused to go when it was needed. The doctor on call, however, took issue with the fact that they'd had a home birth. In his annoyed state, he proceeded to simply yank out the placenta, the very thing they were smart enough to know *not* to do at home. Thank God, in this particular case it didn't create serious problems, but it's a good example of how resentment of another person or their choices can cloud good judgment and provoke someone to do something foolish and even dangerous. The best part of this story is that mama chose to immediately forgive, and as a result, by the next day she reaped the harvest of receiving entirely different treatment from the same people than when she was initially admitted. Forgiving also kept her free to move forward in future births, rather than being tied to trauma and bitterness over what was wrongly done to her.

The bottom line is that any birth worker, if motivated by anything other than what's absolutely best for mom and baby, can't be fully trusted to make the right calls. Sometimes the people harboring these wrong motives don't even fully realize what they're doing or what is driving them, which in some ways makes it even more dangerous. Anyone working in birth should be checking their heart on a regular basis to make sure their motives remain pure and they're allowing the wisdom of God to lead them. It could mean life or death to someone.

To experience birth as God intended, without any fear involved, one of the most counterproductive things you can do is hire a medical care provider or any other birth worker who is allowing fear to dictate how they do their work. Not only does the absence of fear in your heart matter, but also the absence of fear in those around you.

As found in Genesis 35:17, one of the most crucial and effectual roles of those who attend women in labor and birth is to be a voice of love saying, "Do not fear!" The best way to see who is doing that is to judge by the standard of love found in I Corinthians 13. It describes exactly what love is and does, as well as what it is not and does not do, making it quite easy to discern someone's love walk.

If they put their own comfort and convenience before yours, that's not love.

If they shame or belittle you, purposely making you feel stupid, that's not love.

If in the moments when you most need comfort and compassion they instead raise their voice, scold and lecture, become irritable or rude, that's not love.

If they demand their way and their way only, that's not love.

If they are prejudiced against you, whether due to race, social status, age, marital status, etc., that's not love.

If they are prideful know-it-alls whose authority and position can never be questioned, that's not love.

If they do not value and celebrate integrity, that's not love.

If they use fear to manipulate, coerce, or sway you in any direction, that's not love. There is no fear in love. (I John 4:18)

If they want to control your choices or attempt to use force in any way, that's not love.

If they withhold good from you when it's in their power to do, that's not love. (Proverbs 3:27) It's one thing to want to help someone but not have the ability to do so. It's another to be fully capable of helping but choosing not to.

Having a positive provider who walks in love doesn't mean nothing that could potentially be viewed as negative will ever come up. Denial of issues that may arise is not helpful to anyone. However, there is a way to discuss things like risks versus benefits or how to handle possible complications in a loving, faith filled way rather than in fear. You can make fully informed choices without fear being the dictator of what to do.

Walking in love also doesn't mean that no one can ever say anything unfavorable about any other birth worker, system, or model of care in an effort to warn or help someone make a good, safe choice. Sometimes you must tell an uncomfortable truth to protect others. However, you won't tell it in a malicious spirit with the intent to hurt someone. When walking in love, your intent is always to protect.

Now, chances are you won't find a provider who thinks or believes exactly like you do on every point, either naturally or spiritually. More likely than not, you also don't see eye to eye on everything with family or friends whom you may want at your birth. The thing is, you don't necessarily need people who think or do all the same things as you, but who are of the same spirit. II Corinthians 12:18 (NASB), "Titus did not take any advantage of you, did he? Did we not conduct ourselves in the same spirit and walk in the same steps?"

The spirit in which something is said or done largely determines the true intent or meaning of those words or actions.

"Don't you look good today!" That can be said in many different spirits, like a spirit of jealousy, a spirit of self pity, a flattering spirit, a spirit of pride, a scoffing spirit, or a sincere spirit of love and encouragement. Whatever the spirit is in which something is said reveals the purpose for saying it. "You're saying that because…."

If you don't know the Spirit behind God's words, you cannot fully grasp the true meaning of what He says, or you may misinterpret it. You must know that everything God says is said in a spirit of love. His Spirit is not a spirit of slavery or fear, but of freedom, life, power, a sound mind, wisdom, understanding, knowledge, counsel and strength.

Those who walk in that spirit of love are the ones you can trust as a birth team.

When I lived in Texas I was privileged to attend a birth with a renowned, highly sought after doctor in that area. I have yet to see another doctor like him, who so genuinely cared about his clients. With him, it was not just business, or about what would afford him the most convenience and most generously line his pockets. He was known for honoring women's desires in cases that many doctors wouldn't, such as vaginal births after c-sections, vaginal breech births, and vaginal twin births. Even so, as much as I respected him, he did some things differently than I would prefer or think best, such as having mom lie on her back for delivery. However, his decision to walk in the spirit of love, as opposed to a spirit of pride or control, hugely contributed to that being the most peaceful and love filled hospital birth I've witnessed thus far.

A provider-client relationship should be built on mutual trust. Even though the responsibility of choice is rightfully the client's, the provider also has a great responsibility to do their job to the best of their ability and training. As such, the client needs to draw on their expertise and wisdom, doing their best to implement the suggestions and guidance they are given, provided they are evidence based and proven.

Imagine how understandably frustrating it would be as a provider, knowing what action is needed for certain positive results, but having their advice ignored by the client, potentially causing problems or risks that could have been avoided. For example, if they advise that you eat adequate protein, take specific supplements, do certain exercises, and stay properly hydrated, they're telling you those things because they have seen and know the difference it makes. If you don't cooperate, subsequently creating complications, they then have to deal with those problems too, not just you. Just as the provider cannot have a my-way-or-the-highway attitude, the client likewise has to have a listening ear. There must be a mutual respect for the responsibilities of each party, and a realization of potential risks you may be creating for the other person if you don't honor their position.

If the provider is so far from what you believe and desire that you cannot come into agreement and cooperate with anything they say or recommend, why hire them to begin with?

Maybe you didn't realize what your care provider was really like before hiring them, or perhaps the Lord has brought something to your attention that would stand in the way of your desired birth. If you have become uncomfortable and unable to trust them enough to come into true agreement, it's not too late to find another provider. Whoever you hire, you can also fire. There are women who have done so literally in the last week of pregnancy or even when already in labor!

Just as there needs to be agreement between you and your provider, there needs to be harmony among everyone else present at your birth. If your mother or sister or best friend is not on board with the way you have chosen to give birth, it will affect the atmosphere of the room.

For the desires God has placed in you to be realized, they require the right atmosphere of faith and agreement, not only in word but also action, attitude, and even body language. Everyone carries a distinct presence wherever they go. It's not always necessarily that one is better than another, but sometimes it's just not what is good or right for the situation. If someone does not have the same revelation you do about what constitutes safe birth, they will not be able to have faith to agree with you and maintain peaceful harmony in the room. I know you love your mama and your mama loves you, but if she is deathly afraid that you are endangering your baby's life by having an out of hospital birth, it would be better that she wait outside. You do *not* have to give anyone access to your birth space simply out of a sense of obligation.

It is your responsibility to put up a guard against things that may disrupt unity. Ephesians 4:3 (TPT), "Be faithful to guard the sweet harmony of the Holy Spirit among you in the bonds of peace."

In Mark 5:35-43, when He was about to raise a little girl from the dead, Jesus knew that to make room, or create an atmosphere, for the supernatural to take place, the fearful, unbelieving and ridiculing voices had to be put outside. He didn't even allow all his disciples to go into the room with Him, but only the three who were closest to Him.

Were his other disciples bad people? Of course not! Didn't He love them? Of course He did! However, they were not right for this specific moment.

It's ok to be very selective about who you invite into your birth space, whether others understand it or not. What you see and hear from the people present at your birth should agree with the truth you are standing on. If it doesn't, you have the right to put them out. In what is one of the most intense, holy things you'll ever do, you cannot afford to allow anything in your eyes, ears, and heart that will not be life, strength, peace, joy, and encouragement to you.

Have people around you who will make the baby inside you leap, just as the baby in Elizabeth's belly leapt for joy at the sound of Mary's voice! (Luke 1:41)

The Biblical definition of a midwife, which we can take to mean anyone attending women in birth, is someone who helps others bring forth what they have conceived, nurtured, and carried, and to do so safely. The primary ways they do this successfully are through their life giving words, wisdom, and comfort. When thinking of a birth worker who is graced and anointed to do their job, the greatest aspect of God's nature that comes to my mind is comfort. II Corinthians 1:3 says God is the source of all comfort. This word comfort doesn't just refer to feeling sympathy and subsequently attempting to console. Real, God-like comfort is a strengthener, help, and encouragement. The Strong's Concordance tells us the feminine noun "paraklēsis" in II Corinthians 1:3 is also defined as persuasive discourse or stirring address that is instructive and exhorting. It sounds a lot like, *"You can do this!"* The similar masculine noun "paraklētos" in John 14, 15, and 16 is translated as Comforter in description of the Holy Spirit. It's also defined as a help, aid, or assistant called to one's side, and one who pleads another's cause as an advocate or intercessor. I am persuaded that anyone working with or present with women who are giving birth, whether doctors, nurses, doulas, midwives, family, or friends, should be a reflection of this description of comfort, and the Comforter Himself. No one will be 100% faultless in every way, but there are those whose hearts are perfect toward God, and you will see their honor for Him and His ways translate into their work and how they interact with and treat you. You want someone whom Holy Spirit can work through to help, comfort, intercede, counsel, strengthen, and divinely encourage you. You want people who listen for a word from the Lord that will sustain you when you are weary (Isaiah 50:4). You want those who walk in the Spirit of Truth, because the truth is what will be a real help to you.

Integrity is more than not telling a lie. A person of integrity will not willfully lead you on, saying one thing but then doing another, nor withhold truth from you. They will not give you a lethal mixture of truth and lies. Their words and actions match. They are stable, reliable, and consistent, not double minded and shifting, which is completely out of line with God's character. As Proverbs 24:21 (AMP) says, "Do not associate with those who are given to change." Lack of integrity brings disappointment.

Remember, God wants you satisfied!

9 natural things matter too

"Now may the God of peace Himself sanctify you completely; and may your whole spirit, soul, and body be preserved blameless at the coming of our Lord Jesus Christ." I Thessalonians 5:23 (NKJV)

It is essential that we understand we are triune beings. We are spirits, who have a soul, and live in a body. Your spirit is the inner, real you, while your soul is made up of your mind, will, and emotions.

The intended, perfect order of these three areas is spirit first, soul second, and body third.

While they do have this order of importance and priority, all three parts affect the others. They are inseparable. No one part of your being is completely self isolated. They are all created by God, and as such, He intended that they work together in harmony. Yet, failing to connect the dots, people often don't see how neglecting any one part can affect the others, and end up finding themselves in less than desirable circumstances, whether it be primarily in the area they've most neglected, or, because all are connected, in one or more of the others as well.

For example, you could see negative effects of a malnourished spirit or unstable soul in the physical body. In other cases, you may see a well nourished body have a positive effect on the soul.

Think of yourself in terms of a three legged stool. If any one of the three legs is weak or damaged, it creates potential for pain and injury when weight is put on the stool.

Neglecting or undervaluing the natural, physical realm doesn't somehow increase the percentage of us that is spirit, making us more spiritual. You don't become spiritually stronger by ignoring the needs and design of your physical body.

Only the nourishment and exercise of any given area is what makes that particular area strong.

When you nourish your spirit with high quality spiritual food and join action to faith, you become spiritually strong.

When you nourish your body with high quality natural food and exercise it, you become physically strong.

This goes for the soul as well. On the flip side, if you keep filling your mind with trash it should be no surprise if you struggle to remain mentally and emotionally stable and strong.

In order for our experience of pregnancy, birth, and life in general to be the best it can be, we must embrace the natural, physical things in this world as being just as much set in place by God as the spiritual. We must give necessary, adequate consideration to natural laws and principles, without ignoring spiritual laws and principles. We must learn what governs our environment and physical bodies, and what they are designed to need in order to function optimally, as God originally, and still, intended and desires.

Consider the fact that in Eden, the spirituality of mankind was completely sound, whole, and perfect due to unbroken relationship with God. Surely nothing in the natural could make that scenario any better could it? Well, although Adam talked and walked in the Garden with God Himself, God still called him "alone". What?? But...but... he's so spiritually perfect! How could he need or even want anything else?

You see, often we view natural things as an enemy to conquer, or a distraction from more "real" spiritual things. Yet, the natural doesn't need to be crushed or overthrown. It needs to be restored to original intent and its appropriate place in the order of priority, just like the spiritual.

For many in the body of Christ there seems to be a mistaken idea that giving any attention to natural things automatically demonstrates a lack or decline of spirituality, failure to trust God, or the presence of fear. While focusing on the natural *only* certainly can and does allow fear in, to ignore natural things doesn't necessarily mean you're *not* in fear. Some actually close their eyes to what is necessary and beneficial in the natural *because* they are fearful. It may be fear of responsibility, fear of change, fear of being confronted with truth, or fear of failing. Maybe it's a fear of being seen as that weirdo who, because of your choices for a healthy diet and lifestyle, goes against the grain of mainstream society or even your closest family and friends. It may be fear of being misunderstood. It may be fear of facing that what you were taught all your life or thought you knew was actually wrong. It may also be fear of giving up things your flesh really likes, fear of enjoyment and pleasure being taken from you, or fear of it being too hard. One thing is certain: scorning or disregarding the natural is no definitive indication of spiritual maturity nor absence of fear.

Yes, spiritual can and does supersede natural. Spiritual even has the power to change natural. However, if God also created all natural laws, how can we act like they're not relevant in determining outcomes in our lives? Too often Christians can over spiritualize things to the point that we simply overlook or flat out ignore what is good and necessary in the natural.

The story of Daniel in the Bible is a perfect example of how vital it is to walk in knowledge and excellence not only in spiritual matters, but also natural. In the minds of the king and his officials, Daniel was chosen for royal service based on the natural realm only. The king was not a spiritually mature man having a personal relationship with God and being consciously led by the Spirit to choose spiritual giants. His criteria was entirely natural. They had to be good looking, intelligent, quick to learn, strong, physically healthy, and competent to serve in the palace. Yet, this natural criteria was God's door of access to more.

Daniel 1:17 clearly tells us that it was God alone who gave Daniel and his friends their keen intellect, unusual aptitude for learning, wisdom, and skill. Yet, these were obviously not just spiritual attributes seen only in the spiritual realm. Furthermore, in order for them to become visible to the king and world, these guys had to do something *in the natural*. They had to pick up a book and study. They had to apply themselves to learning. They had to stay physically fit, strong and healthy. For God to be able to do in and through their lives all He wanted, they had to be engaged in spirit, soul (the mind, will, and emotions), *and* body. As they embraced and developed their natural, God-given gifts and abilities, as well as maintained a strong spiritual relationship with God, the spiritual and natural united to work together. As a result, God was able to do something far greater through them than just showcase their academic excellence and physical fitness. It was only then that the king and all the people saw the spiritual power that had been involved all along.

Another example of the importance of both natural and spiritual is found in the story of Gideon in Judges 6-7. Gideon was instructed by the Lord to lead an army against an enemy who had been severely oppressing the people of Israel. When the Spirit of God came on him, he had thirty two thousand men summoned to gather for battle. After they arrived, however, the Lord had him narrow the number down to just three hundred men. What was this culling process based on? The first sifting revolved around a seemingly more spiritual matter, as the Lord instructed Gideon to tell anyone who was fearful to go back home. However, the ten thousand who remained had yet to pass one more test. This time it was more about how they would handle and give attention to natural matters. As they came to a water source, the Lord told Gideon that all those who knelt down to drink were to go home, while those who brought the water up to their mouths in their hands were to stay. It has been observed that this revealed who was truly alert and aware of their natural surroundings, because by lowering yourself all the way into the stream to drink you could be caught off guard. Here's the point: the ten thousand who remained after the first cut may have smugly thought, "Yea, we're super spiritual and strong because we're not afraid like those other guys." Yet, lack of excellence in something *natural still* got nine thousand and seven hundred of them sent home.

Throughout their many physical, natural battles against their enemies, the Israelites quickly learned that without God on their side they couldn't win. Certain times they'd mistakenly size up the situation in the natural only and think, "we got this", going on to be completely devastated on the battle field because they had not consulted with God or followed His lead. Other times, when it looked literally humanly impossible to win, they'd have landslide victories! Being outnumbered by the tens of thousands became of no issue when God was fighting with and for them, empowering their physical efforts and giving them success. You see, even while *they* had to do something in the natural, the victory was never determined by natural means alone. You can do everything that you should do in the natural, which is a good thing, but you still need God working with you for it to be truly fruitful and have the maximum effect.

Psalm 127:1a (TPT) says, "If God's grace doesn't help the builders, they will labor in vain to build a house." It doesn't say the builders don't have to work at all. It means you should recognize, acknowledge, and trust God as the source of even your natural ability, knowledge, and success.

We must do with excellence what we can do, while simultaneously trusting God to do what we cannot do!

Luke 16:10-11 (AMP) says, "He who is faithful in a very little thing is also faithful in much; and he who is dishonest in a very little thing is also dishonest in much. Therefore if you have not been faithful in the use of earthly wealth, who will entrust the true riches to you?"

This passage clearly reveals that the natural, which in this context is money, is less important and weighty than the spiritual. However, rather than being entirely disconnected from spirituality, it's actually a testing ground for what you can be trusted with in weightier, spiritual matters. What if Daniel had not been faithful to develop and excel in the natural gifts and talents he'd been given? Do you think he would still have received all the supernatural, spiritual revelation he did? According to Luke, his faithfulness was proven in lesser, earthly, worldly, natural things, which demonstrated how he would handle greater, heavenly things.

Spiritual revelation and understanding, righteousness, and godliness are obviously of much more value than physical fitness, bodily health, and learning to cooperate with our physical design and function. However, if we act like the latter are subjects too petty to give attention to, isn't that rather revealing of whether we really believe that the little things do matter, as stated in Luke 16?

If we refuse to align something so small and seemingly insignificant as our diet with God's original intent and design, how can we expect to be ready and willing to align ourselves with His intent in much greater, weightier areas?

What do we reveal about our hearts if we refuse to educate ourselves on the wonderfully marvelous workmanship that knit us together, due to a belief that such knowledge is too trivial in the big picture of spirituality?

Aiming for excellence in the natural realm is not a dismissal of the spiritual, but rather a declaration that we are committed to faithfulness, which is being true to original intent, in little, less important areas, so that we can be trusted with greater, more important spiritual treasures! This has nothing to do with trying to earn God's love, salvation, approval, or any free gift His grace has made available. It has to do with growing up into maturity, and reaching our potential, as our minds are ever renewed to think as God thinks and be imitators of Him. (Ephesians 4:15b) He is faithful not only in big, spiritual matters, but in little, natural matters as well. If He were not, the very universe itself would instantly fall apart!

I cannot imagine Jesus, on earth as a man, being sloppy in His natural work as a carpenter. I bet His craftsmanship and customer service were so excellent that there was a waiting list for His services. I can't imagine Him being too lazy to take the responsibility of learning natural things that would improve His skills and expand His knowledge base so that He could better serve people. I also can't imagine that He would have purposely put things in His body that were counterproductive to His natural design, hampering His ability to function at His best.

The Bible tells us He *grew*, *became* strong, and *increased* in wisdom. It was a learning, growing process.

Because He was fully human as we are, perhaps He occasionally miscalculated measurements when building a piece of furniture, or discovered easier, better construction methods that would result in an improved product.

Learning something new doesn't always mean you were initially wrong. For example, if I take a specific approach to diet or exercise, believing it's what is best for me, but later learn there's a better way, that doesn't mean I was necessarily wrong in what I was doing previously. I simply need to have the humility and courage to change things I get revelation about on the journey.

Could it be that Jesus' faithfulness in natural matters for thirty years helped prepare him for his ministry of three years?

Recently, I attended a birth where baby had to be resuscitated and spent nine days in the NICU. The placenta had delivered right on the heels of baby, meaning it had detached too early and he was not receiving adequate oxygen through the cord in the last few minutes of birth. This mama had done everything right in the natural. She had applied herself to extensive research and education, eager to learn all she could to be prepared, even before conceiving. She was healthy, fit, and implemented the suggestions and advice of her midwives for her physical well being. She was also strong spiritually, having a solid belief system, and consistently feeding on the truth of the Word for her pregnancy and birth. Throughout her pregnancy I thought to myself, because of her faithfulness to prepare in every area, I *know* her labor and birth will be amazing. I'd seen the difference it makes before. Indeed, her entire pregnancy was healthy and uneventful, and labor went smoothly and quickly, especially for a first time mom.

Now, at first glance, to some it may look like all her education and preparation was in vain, seeing as a baby in the NICU was not what they expected or believed for. I beg to differ. What if she had not educated herself and applied that knowledge so thoroughly, in spirit, soul, and body? Could it be that her faithfulness in *every* area gave God full access to work supernaturally on their behalf? We have no idea of the extent to which further complications were prevented. Not only that, she and her husband were equipped to respond correctly to the turn of events. They remained strong and unwavering throughout, putting their full trust in the Lord to do what absolutely could not be done in the natural!

What if the midwives, who were also believers and loved the Lord, would have had a sloppy approach in their training due to a belief that God will do whatever He wants, that natural excellence is irrelevant, and final outcomes are strictly determined by the spiritual state of matters? "Well, if there's a problem, God will take care of it, so it's not that big a deal if we don't keep our midwifery skills sharp." What if the paramedic team likewise was not at the top of their game? What if everyone's attitude had been that if God wants to save this baby He will, no matter what we do, or don't do, or how fast or slow we move? What if they had tried to make it strictly spiritual, neglecting what was needed in the natural?

Am I implying that any of these people get the credit or glory for saving this baby's life, or that it was all thanks to what was done in the natural? Never! However, did all these people involved apply themselves and their knowledge in the natural, physical realm, just like Daniel, Gideon's men, the Israelite army, and countless others throughout the Word? Absolutely, and they did so with excellence! At the very same time, we watched God do what no amount of natural effort could have accomplished. Anyone involved in this situation with an inkling of an open heart knew without a doubt that throughout it all, God was working with them. The midwife said she'd never seen such an adept, competent paramedic team in twenty-eight years! The doctor said he'd never seen such a miraculous recovery in twenty years! Naturally speaking, the potential for damage to his brain and other organs was drastically high, but every test came back with perfect results! Multiple neurological issues the doctors fully expected to see just weren't there! While God worked through natural people and used natural means, the final outcome of a perfectly healthy baby was anything but natural. They may have been able to keep his heart beating, but they were incapable of bringing about the complete, miraculous turnaround of his condition that occurred shortly after arrival at the hospital. God gets *all* the glory!

Knowledge of natural design and laws really can be the difference between life and death. Imagine if you didn't know about the law of gravity. Or, what if you knew it existed, but refused to believe it and act correspondingly? You'd be in trouble quick! Can God supernaturally supersede the natural law of gravity? Sure, but living your everyday life with that expectation would be foolishness resulting in an early death.

It's not unspiritual to expect natural laws that God Himself set in place to work as He designed them to work. Pretending the natural creation He ordained doesn't exist doesn't honor Him or benefit you.

Now, does this mean there are never incidents where the work is strictly supernatural, without any natural involvement? Absolutely not! Daniel's deliverance from the lion's den later in his life was completely supernatural. It was not *only* the natural nor *only* the supernatural determining outcomes in his life, and neither diminished the importance or value of the other.

In fact, we should be expecting the supernatural all the time! However, that doesn't give us an excuse to be negligent or indifferent to natural things as if they are completely disconnected from God or our spirituality. Sometimes, the uncomfortable truth is that it's more enjoyable and easy on the flesh to just "spiritualize" something than to apply necessary discipline, knowledge, and wisdom in the natural realm.

No matter how much you love God and how spiritually strong you are, a lack of knowledge and application of that knowledge in the *natural realm* can very well be the hindrance to getting your desired birth experience. Many of the problematic issues we see in pregnancy and birth today are not due to flawed bodies, as we are often led to believe.

Rather, they're the result of not knowing the natural laws that govern our bodies well enough to cooperate with them, causing us to make poor choices because we just didn't know any better. What we don't know *can* hurt us.

Faith does not replace knowledge. The devil works hard to keep us dumb and ignorant, trying to deceive us into thinking that as long as we have faith in God, "God will take care of everything! Just leave it up to Him!" That sounds so spiritual, yet, Hosea 4:6 says God's people are destroyed for a lack of knowledge. It's not for a lack of His love, goodness, protection, or competency to handle a situation. According to this scripture, it's not even always because they lack faith.

Proverbs 19:2a (NASB), "It is not good for a person to be without knowledge."

Proverbs 27:12b (NASB), "The naive proceed and pay the penalty."

Proverbs 11:8a, 9b (NASB), "The righteous is delivered from trouble.... through knowledge the righteous will be delivered."

While these scriptures obviously pertain to spiritual knowledge revealed by the Spirit of God, I also believe they can refer to natural knowledge and understanding obtained through intellect. Again, our natural capacity to learn and understand things comes from God, and therefore cannot be considered entirely separate from God and all spiritual matters. When both natural and spiritual come together, that's when we truly see the whole picture.

I've heard so many stories of women who got a hold of the fact that glorious, fear free birth actually does exist. They get their hopes up, as they should, believing it can happen for them, but then at the end of the day, either due to ignorance or refusal to make choices in agreement with natural laws and principles, undesirable circumstances they wanted to avoid are created and they don't fully see that vision come to pass. They are left disappointed and questioning. "Did I not believe enough? Did I not use my faith correctly? What did I do wrong? I thought God's will for me was a supernatural, satisfying birth? How did fear get in?"

The thing is, it may not be a faith issue, or an issue of not having victory over fear, or a spiritual issue at all. It may simply be a lack of knowledge, understanding, and application of natural things.

What are some examples of that? How can ignorance of the natural, willful or not, affect your birth experience?

You may be praying and believing to avoid a c-section, but are seeing a provider with a 50% c-section rate or planning to birth in a hospital known for its unusually high c-section rates.

You may be believing to avoid specific interventions, but have no understanding of how other interventions that you think you're ok with, and maybe even think you want, can often lead to that specific intervention you really want to avoid.

You are really setting your faith not to tear, but don't know your anatomy well enough to understand which pushing positions most effectively prevent it, nor have you learned how proper nutrition or lack thereof can affect even tissue integrity, nor have you ever read a single study showing the difference in tearing rates between mothers who allow their bodies to lead the pushing phase and those who have been coached to "purple push".

You may be confessing and believing that a big baby will have plenty of space to be born vaginally, but then allow yourself to be subjected to policies that limit your mobility, your freedom to labor upright, and your choice of birthing position, which could increase the space in your pelvis by up to 30%!

Whether it be educating yourself on your body's design and physiological needs, or increasing excellence in other natural areas such as your job, academics, fitness, finances, etc., growth in natural matters not only benefits you, but is actually linked to walking in love towards others, thereby also benefitting them.

I Thessalonians 4:9-12 (AMPC), "But concerning brotherly love [for all other Christians], you have no need to have anyone write you, for you yourselves have been [personally] taught by God to love one another. And indeed you already are [extending and displaying your love] to all the brethren throughout Macedonia. But we beseech and earnestly exhort you, brethren, that you excel [in this matter] more and more, to make it your ambition and definitely endeavor to live quietly and peacefully, to mind your own affairs, and to work with your hands, as we

143

charged you, so that you may bear yourselves becomingly and be correct and honorable and command the respect of the outside world, being dependent on nobody [self-supporting] and having need of nothing."

As laid out in this passage, refusing knowledge and excellence in natural matters will ultimately position you to have to rely on others, sometimes to the point of being a burden to them. Not only are you making things more difficult for the people around you, but it's also to your own hurt, because without development in the natural, you will inevitably find yourself in need. It may be need of physical health, need of finances, need of knowledge necessary to make a good choice, need of someone's trust, or a vast array of other needs. It becomes especially detrimental when you find yourself in situations where, because *you* have not yet become self-sufficient or knowledgable enough, you don't have much choice but to rely on the kind of people who themselves are not very trustworthy and dependable.

Gross ignorance, lack of excellence, or naivety in all things pregnancy and birth certainly doesn't command respect of care providers as I Thessalonians 4:12 speaks of. They can tell exactly who has done some research and who hasn't. Unfortunately, that's also often exactly how they know in which cases they can get away with certain unethical or non evidence based practices.

Sometimes, even providers who are doing their job with the right heart and attitude are, of necessity, forced to take more control than they rightfully should, simply because people are so ill educated, unwilling to learn, or have so severely neglected their physical health that some complications become almost inevitable and intervention becomes almost assuredly necessary.

While none of that is ever a justifiable reason to treat women disrespectfully or do absolutely anything in regard to their body or baby without their full knowledge and consent, we also cannot push all blame for subpar experiences on medical professionals and the system, as though we are nothing but victims.

Rather, we must begin to take the initiative to educate ourselves and excel in the natural realm, as well as in the spiritual! We do not have to be weak or ignorant, but remember, knowledge is only power if acted upon.

God obviously always looks beyond how things appear in the natural realm, but the very same scripture that tells us He looks at the heart also tells us that people, on the other hand, *do* look at the outward appearance. (I Samuel 16:7b NKJV)

II Corinthians 8:21, I Peter 2:12, and Romans 12:17 all speak of taking thought for what is good and right not only in the sight of God, but also men. Because people, for the most part, are observing outward things visible to their natural eyes, doing what is good and right in their sight must, then, largely revolve around not only spiritual things, but also natural things.

By the grace of God and with His help, we will grow and excel both naturally and spiritually, being a big blessing to those around us!

10 learn the basics

Now that we've seen the importance of the natural alongside the spiritual, what are some natural things related to pregnancy, labor, and birth that would be truly useful and practical for us to learn? Are there key areas of education that would help us more than others, or do we have to know everything there is to know, including the ins and outs of every possible complication, available test, and potential medical intervention? Do we have to research everything from nutrition, to episiotomies, circumcision, fetal monitoring, and scores of other associated topics?

First of all, what you will need to research and educate yourself on depends somewhat on where you plan to give birth and what their standard of care looks like, as well as how much knowledge and education they are providing on any given matter.

For the most part, simply having a good foundation in the basics of *normal* anatomy and physiology, which most women in western culture today do not have, provides sufficient understanding of our bodies and the birth process to be well prepared for pregnancy and birth. By narrowing it down to our original design and function, and learning what is natural and normal rather than man-made or abnormal, we can simplify education about our bodies and birth to an easily understandable, non overwhelming, yet extremely helpful, place.

As mentioned in chapter one, to be true to the original intent or plan of a thing, you must know what that original intent is. When we really understand, and then trust God's design of our bodies, we'll do everything in our power to work with, instead of against, that design.

For example, when you understand the design of the female pelvis and how baby must navigate the shape of the pelvis in labor, it's a lightbulb moment that clarifies why you would want to labor and give birth in certain ways and positions. "Oh! If that's how my body is designed then this is what I need to do to support and work with that design!"

The more you believe that every detail of birth was strategically, perfectly planned and designed by a loving Creator, the easier it is to trust the process.

On the other hand, those who are predisposed to view birth as a medical emergency with an underlying belief that natural design is risky and flawed, expecting it to fail and thus require intervention, will rarely, if ever, witness a truly physiological birth.

While certainly not an exhaustive list, some of the chief areas of foundational education in the natural that I believe would be of help to every woman, especially those of childbearing age, include hormonal balance, menstrual cycles and fertility, birth control, diet and nutrition, need for movement, as well as the basic physiology of the female body in pregnancy, labor, and birth. By briefly touching on these topics, I hope it stirs you to delve into further research of your own.

While all the aforementioned are quite closely connected, nutrition and diet really affect them all.

Researchers have said that pregnancy is the most energetically expensive activity the human body can possibly maintain for nine months straight.[4] If energy use in pregnancy were much higher, pregnancy would become unsustainable and damaging to the body.

Despite that, it's considered normal and even expected for women to expend that amount of energy severely undernourished, dehydrated, and without any previous physical training whatsoever. Top it off by acting like women in labor are adequately fueled with nothing but ice chips while their body, specifically the uterine muscle, is working harder than it ever has or ever will. Is it any wonder that so often it seems women's bodies don't have what it takes?

No athlete would run a marathon or compete in an Olympic event without preparing their body. They take months and even years to train, maintaining a diet that meets the nutrient needs that come with building up their body and being able to function at their peak ability on the big day.

Meanwhile, most western pregnancy care providers don't emphasize or provide nutritional education beyond recommending a prenatal multivitamin or increasing calorie intake.

The majority of western women today have never learned to connect the dots between nutrition, or lack thereof, and pregnancy or birth symptoms, complications, or difficulties. They're told that as long as they don't smoke, drink alcohol, eat deli meat or raw sushi *during* pregnancy, that will make all the difference between a truly healthy pregnancy and birth or not. There is little to no mention of what they *should* put in their bodies to sufficiently nourish themselves and their babies.

Yet, research shows that 60% of maternal mortality is preventable, much of which correlates to diseases avoidable with proper nutrition. The condition of your overall health, not just *during* pregnancy but even long before you conceive, undeniably affects your pregnancy and labor.

Ask out-of-the-box questions.

Can nutrition either aid or impede fertility when you're trying to conceive? Because the egg you will conceive with takes about ninety days to fully mature before being released, have you considered how you're nurturing that process?

Can gut health play a role in preventing things like pre-eclampsia or group B strep? Can the absence of yeast even affect tissue integrity, reducing the risk of tearing during birth?

How much extra protein do you need to adequately support the growth of your baby? Can protein intake and choice of foods, even well before pregnancy, also help prevent gestational diabetes or lessen nausea in the first trimester?

How many calories of quality, nutrient dense food do you really need to thrive throughout pregnancy and postpartum, rather than become depleted?

What kinds of foods and supplements help build a strong amniotic sac, which can prevent premature rupture of membranes?

What are some foods that are proven to facilitate easier, faster labors?

I understand that the topic of health and nutrition can seem overwhelming and confusing, especially with the crazy amount of so called healthy ways of eating out there today. For me, just as with birth, when I'm not quite sure whether something is truly good for me or just a passing trend, my go-to question is whether it agrees with original design. What are the foods God created, in the state He created them? Is my food a highly altered version of that? What would my ancient ancestors have eaten, when there was much less sickness and disease? How were foods traditionally prepared in times past? They certainly weren't consuming genetically modified, processed, refined foods full of added chemicals, artificial hormones, preservatives, and lab made ingredients.

Even though it may be impossible and even somewhat illogical to eat exactly as our ancestors did, looking to what's original, or as close to it as possible, is still a great place to start cleaning up your diet.

Diet and nutrition, along with reducing stress by honoring the body's need for adequate movement, real rest, and love filled environments, are possibly the greatest keys to hormonal balance, which in turn will positively affect menstrual cycles and fertility.

Speaking of which, how many women actually grow up having thorough knowledge and understanding of a normal menstrual cycle? Did you, like me, assume that the sum total of a cycle was simply getting your period once a month, virtually unaware of the various phases and their purposes that make up the ongoing, month long cycle?

In a nutshell, the follicular phase of the female cycle begins with menstruation, the shedding of the uterine lining which was built up in preparation for possible implantation of a fertilized egg. During this phase, from the first day of your period up to ovulation, the ovaries are getting ready to release an egg. The ovulatory phase is the release of that egg, followed by the luteal phase, when once again, the uterine lining is being prepared for possible implantation of a fertilized egg. If there's no fertilized egg to implant, the luteal phase ends when you find yourself back in menstruation.

Popular thought, also by which due dates are calculated, is that a normal cycle is twenty-eight days long and a woman ovulates on day fourteen. However, there are actually more women who do *not* have a twenty-eight day cycle than that do, and ovulation could easily be occurring anywhere from day ten to day eighteen, with all variations in timing still being healthy and normal. We are not cookie cutter copies of each other. This is one reason why the idea of exact due dates should be held quite loosely.

Because you only have a fertile window of about twenty-four hours after ovulation, you cannot get pregnant on just any day of the month. That said, intercourse that takes place up to five days prior to ovulation can still result in pregnancy, because that's how long sperm are able to survive inside the female body. You can easily learn to recognize and track ovulation either to avoid conception or to help you conceive.

When we really begin to see that we, as women, are perfectly designed as cyclic beings, we can better honor that design by learning to flow with the rhythms of our cycle, actually facilitating and supporting it. Unless we do this, we'll never achieve the most optimal balance possible in our hormones and bodies.

This brings us to the subject of birth control. Let me preface by saying I am absolutely *not* opposed to controlling how many children one has by way of pregnancy prevention practices. I would also never tell you you're wrong for making a different choice of method than I. I do, however, want women to know the full risks and benefits of something that can be as life altering as hormonal birth control. I also want them to know they have options, rather than wrongfully be told that hormonal birth control *is* their only option. Many women have suffered horrible side effects because they weren't given the truth, being left to wonder what's wrong with themselves. For that reason, I simply want to present some food for thought that is severely lacking from mainstream perspective.

According to the Guttmacher Institute, 58% of women prescribed the birth control pill rely on it, at least in part, for purposes other than pregnancy prevention.[5] Young women have been put on birth control as early as eleven years old, being told that it would fix or manage all their issues from acne, to heavy periods, no periods, painful periods, irregular periods, endometriosis, PCOS, PMS, and more. While some do get much needed symptom relief, how many women or their doctors have stopped to question *why* they are experiencing these symptoms to begin with? There is always a root cause. Hormonal birth control is a bandaid covering up a symptom, but not a true fix of the root cause.

For many, it has ended up costing them more than they had hoped to gain from it. Are depression and anxiety a good, worthy trade for less acne? Is complete hormonal imbalance a fair exchange for a shorter period?

Unbeknownst to most women on the birth control pill, this medication is depleting Vitamin B2, B6, B12, folate, magnesium, zinc, selenium, Vitamin C, and Vitamin E.[6] Often coupled with a diet severely lacking in nutrient density and an overly stressful lifestyle, it's no wonder so many women feel like they're barely keeping their head above water.

On top of that, most women don't even really know how hormonal birth control actually works to prevent pregnancy, as revealed in a message I once received from a young woman trying to conceive:

"I came off the patch five months ago and have only had a period a few times. I haven't had one for the past two months. They told me the patch was better than the pill because it wouldn't mess with my system like the pill. All pregnancy tests are coming back negative."

For a care provider to imply that hormonal birth control of *any kind* will not affect your hormones or "system" is completely misleading, because that is exactly what it's fundamentally designed to do. In short, hormonal birth control changes the communication between your brain and ovaries by delivering an unnatural, large dose of hormones that reduces the production of other hormones which would tell the ovaries to get an egg ready and ovulate. It's entire purpose is to *stop ovulation* by affecting your natural hormonal ebb and flow. If it *doesn't* prevent ovulation by doing that it has *failed*!

You may be wondering, "If I don't want to get pregnant anyway, then it shouldn't matter whether or not I ovulate, right?" The idea that ovulation is unnecessary if not trying to conceive may be popular, but in reality, ovulation is always a good thing.

Not ovulating creates hormonal imbalance because without ovulation, you're not able to produce sufficient amounts of progesterone. Without adequate progesterone, estrogen levels are left unchecked, and you're likely to find yourself in estrogen dominance. Estrogen dominance is not

155

always a result of your body making too much estrogen, but often a result of not producing enough progesterone to counter balance it.

Healthy, strong fertility, which is impossible without healthy, strong cycles, is one of the greatest markers of women's health. Without ovulation you're not having a true cycle, as the greatest purpose of a full monthly cycle is actually ovulation, and not just getting a period. In fact, while on the pill, the periodic or monthly bleeding you may experience is not even a real period, but rather a medication withdrawal bleed. Ovulation and a real period are part of a cycle that, when on the pill, has been disrupted and broken.

An imbalanced body is not a truly happy, fully functioning body. The effects of imbalance can show up mentally, emotionally, and physically. Imbalance created by low progesterone and high estrogen can cause symptoms such as anxiety, depression, PMS, irregular, heavy, or painful periods, difficulty getting pregnant, higher risk of miscarriage, headaches or migraines, trouble sleeping, hair loss, weight gain, breast swelling and tenderness, low libido, mood swings, irritability, memory problems and mental fog, hot flashes and night sweats, reduced energy and fatigue. Interestingly, many actually start using hormonal birth control because they are already experiencing these symptoms of imbalance, being led to believe that it will bring them back into balance, while it actually only takes them into further imbalance. For others, imbalance is caused largely by the birth control itself, although they may not immediately see symptoms when beginning its use. Some experience the most severe symptoms only once they *stop* using it, which is also often when they're trying to conceive, a time in which it's especially crucial to be properly balanced and healthy.

Most likely at this point you're asking the ultimate question: "But what if I don't take birth control and then get pregnant??"

While I am totally in favor of responsible family planning, I believe if we were honest we'd have to acknowledge that by and large, most aversion to unplanned pregnancy is rooted in fear. It's not usually simply about not wanting to have a baby, but about fear stemming from the circumstances surrounding the conception or raising of that child.

Fear is never from the Lord. It's never helpful or healthy. It should never be the motivation for our choices, even our choice of pregnancy prevention method.

What are some reasons women might live in constant fear of getting pregnant?

Are they in a harmful relationship they need to get out of?

Are they sexually active with someone they don't think would stay and be a real father if they got pregnant?

Are they afraid of the financial implications?

Are they afraid they're incapable of being a good parent?

Are they afraid it would ruin their chances of a successful career?

Are they afraid their marriage wouldn't survive it?

Now, if you are inside the safeguards of a healthy, happy marriage, perhaps questions like these are even more pertinent. Is it worse to have a baby who adds joy and meaning to your life than to live a severely decreased quality of life due to perpetual mood disorders, anxiety, depression, uncontrollable weight gain, constant health issues, and never feeling like your true self?

Are we allowing the enemy to create such intense fear around unplanned pregnancy that we will go to the point of seriously damaging our bodies and health with hormonal birth control, convinced that having a baby "at the wrong time" would completely mess up our life?

While this may not sound like your personal experience while on birth control, for many, this is their world, even if perhaps they've never connected the dots.

I certainly understand there are seasons in life when it would seem completely inconvenient and even challenging to have a baby. I totally get it if you're not inclined toward having Irish twins. I know there comes a time when you feel like you're done having babies, and a surprise pregnancy doesn't sound very exciting. Again, I'm not advocating for using no prevention methods whatsoever, nor trying to guilt-trip anyone if you're in one of those seasons when you just don't desire a baby.

I believe one reason many are largely motivated to use hormonal birth control no matter what the cost is because they've come to believe the widely spread message that it's the only reliable and effective pregnancy prevention method, and without it you will automatically get pregnant in no time at all. This is absolutely not true! Other non hormonal options include diaphragms, sponges, condoms, cervical caps, spermicides, the withdrawal method, and of course, more permanent measures like tubal ligations and vasectomies. Many of these methods can be used in conjunction with others. On top of all that, and perhaps one of the most reliable, you can learn to track your monthly ovulation and fertile window, thereby knowing exactly when you could get pregnant and when not. This fertility awareness method in and of itself is 95-99% effective with correct use.

The truth is, there's not one single birth control method that is 100% effective at all times, not even a vasectomy or getting tubes tied. If that's what you're looking for, total abstinence is your only option! This highlights the point that if you want to be sexually active, you should also be ready for the possibility and privilege of becoming a parent, whether or not that actually happens.

As for the normal physiology of the female body in pregnancy, labor, and birth, this area of education will not only help you see which choices best support you and your baby, it will also flat out amaze you, starting with the process of conception, implantation, and development of baby! Here are just a few fun facts to scratch the surface and pique your interest!

In just the first twelve, short weeks every organ and part of your baby's body is already present, from which time they simply continue to develop in size and function. That might explain why you're so exhausted and hungry in the first trimester; your body has been working nonstop!

During pregnancy your blood volume is increasing by up to 50%! You might want to find out how you can nutritionally support that drastic increase.

The female pelvis, which boasts the strongest joints in the body, is shaped and designed specifically for giving birth, unlike a male's. The pregnant body increases flexibility and mobility in these joints via pregnancy hormones in order to create the maximum amount of space for baby during birth. Laboring and pushing positions greatly affect how freely these joints and bones are able to move and adjust, either minimizing or maximizing the amount of available space by up to 30%!

As long as they have sufficient, balanced space, your baby knows exactly how to position themself most favorably for the easiest exit. They instinctively tuck their chins and rotate their way through the pelvis, presenting the smallest diameters of their head first, and aligning the widest part of their head and shoulders with the widest parts of both the pelvic inlet and the pelvic outlet.

You can also be proactive in helping baby get into optimal position for labor by giving attention to the balance and alignment of your muscles, ligaments, and bone structure, as those can largely affect the amount of available space for baby and their ability to best position themselves. Baby being head down is not the only positional factor necessary to consider. This is just one area in which chiropractic care, appropriate exercise and movement can be helpful.

Contractions work to produce dilation, effacement, and descent of baby. Dilation refers to how much the cervix has opened, measured in centimeters from 0-10. Effacement refers to how much the cervix has thinned and stretched, from 0-100%. Station refers to how high or low the baby's presenting part is in the pelvis, with -3 being highest and +3 lowest. You may want to question whether it's always beneficial to know all these numbers during labor, or whether there are other, additional ways to gauge labor progress.

If you are planning for a hospital birth or medical interventions, for the best possible experience, it's also important to learn some basic medical terms, hospital protocol, common medical procedures related to labor and birth, and the risks and benefits of any interventions being considered.

When contemplating an intervention, understanding not only what it's meant to achieve, but also how it's performed, can be extremely helpful in your decision making process. Most women have heard about epidurals, inductions, cesareans, episiotomies, artificial rupture of membranes, and more, but many don't really know how any of these things are actually carried out.

For example, at one birth I attended, it seemed this mama had somehow picked up the mistaken idea that she was not truly in labor until her water was broken. For that reason, she was very eager to have it done artificially early on in the induction process. However, once the doctor began the procedure, I realized she was completely unprepared for what it entailed. I guess she didn't know that it meant pushing an amnihook all the way up through her cervix. This was very painful and stressful to her. She sobbed as I did my best to talk her through it and explain what was being done, which no one else in the room even attempted to do. Perhaps the saddest part was that this was a completely unnecessary intervention that she herself requested, thinking it was what she wanted, but without really understanding what was involved.

When women don't know the physiological design of birth, they can be very easily led to believe certain situations are abnormal or constitute an emergency, making interventions necessary, when they really are not.

For example, most women don't know that their water actually doesn't even have to break at all in order to birth their baby. This is called being born "en caul", or in other words, baby is still inside the intact sac full of water. One of my own nephews was born this way! I believe we'd see it a lot more often if artificial rupture of membranes was not so often performed.

However, because facts like this are not well known, moms can easily be talked into having their water broken artificially for a large variety of so called reasons, many of which are not medical. The most bizarre one

I've personally heard was "so it doesn't splash on us". Um, nope, that's not a medical reason!

Learn exactly how an epidural works to eliminate pain, and how it's placed. Be aware that getting an epidural will also require having a bladder catheter placed, among other things perhaps you haven't thought about.

Understand that a c-section is major surgery, cutting through seven layers in your abdomen to get to baby. It's certainly not the easy way out as some think, which is why my hat is off to the women who don't think twice about taking the risk when it's truly necessary.

Learn the difference between Pitocin® and natural oxytocin. Do they both produce the same types of contractions that are well tolerated by baby?

How is an internal monitor attached to your baby still in the womb?

How quickly might your doctor be prone to employ forceps or vacuum extraction?

How is an episiotomy performed?

Did you know that induction can take days, and even then may not be successful?

There are no wrong, dumb, or excessive questions. If something cannot be questioned, that's a red flag.

It's better to ask questions, seek counsel, and get wisdom beforehand than forever afterwards be questioning, "What just happened??"

As you research and educate yourself in all these areas I've mentioned, there are a few things to keep in mind. While I'm all for evidence based research, and I encourage checking whether something is supported by studies, I also feel that if we lean too much in the direction of not believing anything that doesn't have a published study to back it up, we'll miss out on some valuable truths. Anecdotal evidence, which is defined as being based on personal accounts rather than research, cannot be completely dismissed, as though people's very real, personal experiences and observations are all lies. For example, Ina May Gaskin observed that women would sometimes regress or go backward in dilation when they were disturbed, afraid, or unsettled, but there were no studies to prove this and the "notion" was largely dismissed. If telling, physiological clues as to how the mind, brain, and body connect to govern birth are ignored, this becomes detrimental to all women because it affects the standard policies of care in labor and birth.

People's individual judgment, insight, and God-given intuition are often years ahead of studies, perhaps even being what inspire the initiation of many studies. Not only that, but studies are also much farther advanced than currently implemented care policies and practices. On average it takes about seventeen years for evidence to be put into practice and health care to make large policy shifts, even if the data has been there all along.[7] Additionally, even the studies can be flawed. For all these reasons and more, we don't always have to wait for a published study, and then wait until that study is actually reflected in common practice before we can make choices that we know are right for us and our children.

So yes, look at the studies. There are many great ones that if acted on, would change some disadvantageous, yet still popular, ways of doing things. But don't stop there, and don't lean entirely on studies alone.

I'm not talking about believing just anything anyone says either. I know for myself, I was told so many myths and old wives' tales when I was pregnant and having babies it was downright ridiculous. Occasionally, however, there were nuggets of truth that I could never have found in any study.

In all your education and research, no matter your sources of information, you must lean on the Holy Spirit to lead you into *all* truth!

11 have a vision & be led

As I'm sure you're beginning to see, education, planning, and preparation, both in spiritual and natural matters, is essential in preventing fear from having any place in your pregnancy and birth.

Solid plans and preparation for pregnancy, birth, and beyond will be founded on both information *and* revelation.

They cannot be built only on doing the best we know, but also on what's been revealed to us by the Holy Spirit, having ears to hear from Him all along the way. One of the Holy Spirit's jobs is to show us things to come, and He does this so that we *can* prepare for it.

At the same time, that doesn't mean we have to know every exact detail of how something is going to transpire in order to be ready for it. If we did, living by faith would become irrelevant.

Proverbs 31:21 (NASB), "She is not afraid of the snow for her household, for all her household are clothed with scarlet." The reason she's not afraid is because her household is ready for what's coming. She may not know exactly which day it will start snowing, or how much it will snow, or how long it will snow, but she does know it will snow and therefore she has prepared for it.

In Joshua 1, Israel was instructed to prepare for their imminent entrance into the Promised Land. They were told exactly where they were going and what the mission was. Then in chapter 3:4, they were given a very specific distance at which to follow the Ark of the Covenant, which represented the Presence of God and was carried by the priests ahead of the people as they entered the land. "Do not come near it, that you may know the way by which you shall go, for you have not passed this way before." (NASB) So although they had prepared, had a plan, knew the destination and what the final outcome was to be, they *still* had to follow the presence to know how to get there. They had to stay far enough behind that they could clearly see which way it was going in order to be led by it.

For original intent to be seen, the individual, personal leading of the Holy Spirit cannot be discounted or overlooked.

"Plans succeed through good counsel." (Proverbs 20:18a NLT) He is our ultimate Counselor!

Thorough preparation for birth includes the preparation of your heart.

Psalm 10:17a (NKJV), "Lord, You have heard the desire of the humble; You will prepare their heart." The word prepare here means to strengthen, establish, build up, furnish, ready, stabilize, and be enduring. Why is it so important that this happens?

If your heart is not prepared, you may grow weary in the faith journey that leads to the fulfillment of the vision in your heart.

"And let us not grow weary while doing good, for in due season we shall reap if we do not lose heart." Galatians 6:9 (NKJV)

The reason people give up on the vision God gave them, or start wondering if it's worth the effort, is because they begin to doubt they will reap. They begin to wonder if they will see the goodness of God or be able to enjoy the harvest from the seeds they've sown.

"I would have lost heart, unless I had believed that I would see the goodness of the Lord in the land of the living. Wait on the Lord; be of good courage, and He shall strengthen your heart; wait, I say, on the Lord!" (Psalm 27:13-14 NKJV)

When you begin to lose heart, everything more easily seems wearying, exhausting and spiritless. When fatigue walks in, faith walks out.

Proverbs 18:14 (AMPC) describes it like this, "The strong spirit of a man sustains him in bodily pain or trouble, but a weak and broken spirit who can raise up or bear?"

A weak and weary heart does not have much endurance. Yet, Hebrews 6:12 says it's through faith *and* patience that we inherit the promises.

How, then, is the Lord able to prepare your heart according to Psalm 10:17? It's when you commit to feeding your faith by hearing what the will of God is for you, which is found in His Word and through personal communication with Him.

As you develop your spiritual ears, learning to hear and recognize the Lord's voice and direction more and more clearly, you'll also learn to differentiate between fear and warnings, and between feigned faith and real faith. Real faith does not just claim to stand on the Word while simultaneously ignoring personal direction God is giving you. In fact, it's impossible for you to have faith for something you haven't heard from God about, and especially not if you've heard a word that's different or opposite of what you claim to be believing. For example, you cannot have faith for a successful home birth if the Lord has directed you to have a hospital birth, and the same vice versa.

In conversation after one of the breech births I attended, we found that all of us - parents, midwives, and myself - when praying over this birth, couldn't really bring ourselves to pray that he would turn, but rather, simply that he would be in the right position *for him*. Had we just ignored that sense we all had and prayed for him to turn we wouldn't have been praying in faith anyway, because that's not how we were being *led* to pray. Then when it didn't happen, people could have mistakenly assumed that "faith doesn't always work", when in reality, it was never real faith to begin with. It would have been groundless, having no word to stand on.

The truth is, sometimes breech *is* the position a baby needs, and the Lord knows exactly when that is! He was born strong and healthy, but who knows what kinds of complications may have arisen if he *had* turned. That was the position *right* for *him* just like we had prayed!

Not only must your heart be prepared, you must also guard it by giving ear only to faith filled, life giving words, controlling what gets into your heart through the gates of your eyes and ears.

"Keep and guard your heart with all vigilance and above all that you guard, for out of it flow the springs of life." (Proverbs 4:23 AMPC)

You cannot allow negative, faithless, and discouraging voices to speak into your life. There are many people with many words which, if they get in your heart, will counterproductively produce fear.

Whatever it is that you really want to believe and see come to pass, that's what you're going to have to be hearing!

You may get criticized for this kind of extreme prioritization, because many do not understand the amount of focus it takes to properly prepare for birth or anything else significant. They don't understand that preparation actually requires as much focus and prioritization as the actual doing of whatever it is you're preparing for. You must be like a racehorse wearing blinkers, tuning out all that distracts you from the vision you're focused in on.

When your heart is established, prepared, and guarded, you are able to catch and keep God's vision for your birth.

In the birth arena, the vision is often referred to as a birth plan or birth preferences. Being somewhat of a controversial topic, some say that because so much about birth cannot be planned, planning sets you up for disappointment. Others say if you don't have a plan detailing exactly what you want, you're unlikely to get it.

I like to say there's a difference between planning every detail and having a clear, definite vision based on what you know is God's best for you. Rigid over planning absolutely can result in disappointment, frustration, and even damaged faith, because it can tend to choke out any room to be individually led by the Spirit. However, under preparing due to a lack of vision can also give way to deeply disheartening, unpleasant circumstances or outcomes. We must simply ask what really matters enough to fight the good fight of faith for, while remembering that a change of plans does not equal failure.

Let's say that you, as a planner on steroids, have planned every detail of your birth experience down to a tee — sibling outfits for the perfect photos, flawless makeup, hair, and nails, the most beautifully prepared birth space, your mom flying in to be present for the birth, your whole team on speed dial, a meticulously cleaned house on the big day, and on it goes. Then you end up having a whirlwind, precipitous birth two weeks early in middle of the night, having no time or even concern for your appearance and that cute robe you carefully picked out. The night before you fell into bed exhausted thinking, "I'll have time to clean tomorrow", and the kids come stumbling in sleepy eyed in their pj's to meet the baby before the photographer even arrives. You never lit one of those candles or turned on that curated playlist or even thought about trying to get the birth pool filled. As you can see, in this sense, it's true that birth very often doesn't go to plan, and it's not wise to set your heart too intently on an exact scenario that could very easily look different.

However, we still cannot be so heavily inclined to think that because birth is unpredictable, it's pointless to have a vision, as if we have no control over the process and outcome, and simply have to accept *whatever* happens.

Depending on which translation you look at, Proverbs 29:18 says that where there is no vision, people perish, run wild, wander astray, or cast off restraint. Having a vision helps keep you grounded, focused, safe, and successful!

But what if an unexpected change of plans affects something far more significant than what you're wearing or whether you get good birth photos?

The sixth birth I ever attended was one of the most profound for me personally. I witnessed firsthand how derailed plans can't automatically dictate environment, peace, attitude, or final outcome if you don't let them. This was another breech baby, and these first time parents were planning for a birth center birth. While midwives in that state could legally attend breech births, her midwives were uncomfortable doing so. Labor began around 12:30 AM. Around 6:00 AM, mom was checked at the birth center one more time to see if baby may have flipped. He hadn't, and mama had already dilated to six centimeters, so off to the hospital we all went, where a backup doctor was willing to attend vaginal breech birth. As you can tell, right off the bat it seemed things weren't going "as planned". However, instead of immediately yielding to the temptation to believe, "nothing is working" (Remember, we've been redeemed from the curse of nothing working.), they kept their peace and faith that she would have a great labor, everything would work together for their good, and they would have a healthy, strong baby. As the day went on, progress slowed considerably. Sometime that afternoon, the doctor came in and kindly broached the subject of possibly needing some kind of intervention if things didn't start to pick up pace shortly. Baby and mom were doing well, but one concern was that mom would simply get too exhausted to finish if it took too long, especially because she had gotten almost no sleep the night before.

Right then and there, mom and dad began to pray in the spirit, seeking the Lord's wisdom. Everyone in the room paused and respectfully gave them the time and space to do this, some even joining them in prayer. When they finished, the doctor himself commented, "They've done what they needed to do." We then went to work in the natural to encourage stronger contractions that would labor baby down effectively and make faster progress, but again, the natural and spiritual worked hand in hand. As we headed down the hall to walk and squat through contractions, we received words from the Lord to speak over her body. Immediately we began to say what He said, and by our second trip down the long hallway we started to see exactly what we said — contractions that were "longer, stronger, and closer together"!

All day long, every time they had an opportunity to become discouraged, they refused to let go of the promises and supernatural help they knew were theirs. After many hours of labor, when everyone else was already in desperate need of a nap, mom still wasn't even feeling tired!

Finally, around midnight, she was ready to push. During delivery, once again they had opportunity to get sidetracked in fear as baby's head momentarily seemed stuck. Once again, the situation was met with prayer in the spirit and words of faith, and was resolved within seconds. After about twenty-four hours of labor, at 12:33 AM, just like they had believed, planned, and prepared for, she vaginally birthed her healthy, breech baby boy, with some energy left to boot!

While multiple things from start to finish were not necessarily what they had planned or envisioned, they refused to give in, give up, or let go of the things that mattered most, which to them were a peaceful environment, minimal intervention, a successful vaginal birth, and a healthy baby and mom in spirit, soul, and body, which can be summed up as a trauma free birth. I believe this was their experience for the reasons that their hearts were prepared, they didn't give fear or despair a chance despite changes of plans, and they were surrounded by loving, respectful people who were truly supportive.

I tell this story to demonstrate that when things don't go exactly to plan, especially as people of faith, we don't just throw our hands up and act like everything's out of our control. There's always *something* in your control, starting with your response to a turn of events. You can choose to stay in faith for the desired outcome or you can yield to discouragement and just passively let the tide take you where it may.

While having a vision is huge, knowing *what* you want *alone* is not necessarily enough if you're not also equipped with understanding on what might hinder, help, or derail the fulfillment of your desires. Learning what you want and why you want it is the necessary first point, but without acquiring wisdom for clear strategies and steps of implementation, it's often not sufficient to achieve the desired outcome.

God has not only redeemed our ability to make the best choices through revelation knowledge, but, as a very key part of our redemption, has also given us the wisdom on how to apply that knowledge correctly.

Proverbs 4:7 tells us that wisdom is the principal thing, and if we love and prize her, she will keep, defend, protect and guard us.

Proverbs 1:33 and 3:21-26 detail how acquiring the wisdom of God is also linked to freedom from fear. When you have the wisdom of God, you have supernatural insight, and simply receiving that kind of inside information about a situation has the power to strip the fear away. Why would I fear when I know I've received the word of the Lord on something?

According to Proverbs 3:17 (NLT), wisdom also creates the Eden-like conditions of delight and satisfaction. "She will guide you down delightful paths; all her ways are satisfying."

James 1:5 instructs us to ask God for wisdom, promising He will give it generously and without fault finding.

The Holy Spirit Himself, who is our guide into truth, is called the Spirit of wisdom, understanding, and knowledge in Isaiah 11:2.

The story of my third birth as I shared in chapter four is a good example of the difference between only knowing what you want, and also having wisdom on how to obtain it.

For example, I knew I didn't want to be stuck in a bed, but I didn't know *how* to best facilitate that. I thought my goal of remaining mobile and upright would be met by agreeing to an internal monitor. What I didn't realize was that agreeing to have my water broken would so greatly intensify contractions that I wouldn't even *want* to move afterwards. I also didn't know what my other options were, such as intermittent monitoring with a doppler. Had I been familiar enough with the stages of labor or my body's natural labor ryhthms to confidently do so, I could also have prevented early artificial rupture of membranes and limited mobility by laboring at home longer.

Likewise, I knew I didn't want an epidural, but I didn't know exactly *how* to go about labor in such a way that truly would help me realize that vision. A large contributing factor to getting the epidural against my original desire was that I still had somewhat of a "try" mentality, which indicates that I'm not totally sure I have the ability. The environment I was in only reinforced that doubt, as this was also the general feeling I got from staff and the doctor . The "try" mentality is more of a passive approach like: "let's see how it goes". It remains prevalent when there is no specific plan of action on how or what you are going to do to meet the objective. Neither did the staff have any ideas or suggestions to encourage or support a natural labor, nor did I myself have any real, tangible game plan in place.

In my case, the marriage of knowledge and wisdom later resulted in choosing a birthplace and type of care provider who would not always demand compromise and make me fight for what I wanted. For me, that was the only way to truly see my vision come to fruition.

The wisdom of God, which can be seen in original design, always works to keep things pure, peaceful, and uncomplicated. It's the enemy who wants to make things hard and stressful, creating high pressure situations so you'll make hurried, rushed decisions, with the goal of stealing your joy in what should be one of the most joyous times of your life! (Proverbs 19:2)

Planning and preparing for birth and parenthood, while certainly something to be taken seriously and done with intentionality, should be easy and light, not heavy and overwhelming.

If you are feeling pressured or weighed down in your pregnancy, postpartum, or even parenting in general, it's a good idea to evaluate whether it's time to simplify. Ask yourself whether you're trying to carry or implement things that aren't truly necessary.

Have you become married to rules rather than looking for the natural, unforced ryhthms of grace?

Are you more zeroed in on how Grandma did it, the current trend, or that book you read than you are on simply becoming more in tune with Holy Spirit, your baby, and yourself?

Have you been over influenced by all the influencers to the point of feeling pressured to be, buy, and do all the perfect mom things?

One of the greatest misconceptions about simplifying is that it involves sacrificing something valuable, beneficial or even necessary. On the contrary, simplifying is only about removing excess weight and useless clutter that hinders or overwhelms you, which actually ends up *adding* quality to your life. Eliminating the unnecessary allows the necessary to be more clearly seen, enabling you to give your full attention to what matters most.

Simplifying helps clear the noise of a thousand voices so you can hear the Lord's more clearly. It helps you lean in and tune in to Him without distraction.

Even things that should be delightful like preparing a nursery or purchasing all the fun, cute baby things can have the joy sucked right out of them if we start letting ourselves be pressured and ruled instead of led. Honestly, your baby will probably be happiest with a cardboard box, anything involving water, dirt between their toes, maybe a book, and definitely a boob. As with everything else, original design which includes plenty of human interaction, nature, and movement will often be what keep both you and your baby more content and sane than everything else you may have been influenced to think you need. The bottom line is that no tradition, trend, or material item is worth losing your peace or joy over.

My personal breastfeeding journey is a great example of how being led rather than ruled makes things so much easier. It's one of the biggest things I would change if I could do it all over. When I had my first baby, I was taught that if I ever wanted him to sleep through the night or at the least longer than one to two hours at a time, I had to put him on a strict feeding schedule. The goal was to stretch the time between feedings during the day which would supposedly result in longer feeding intervals during the night, with the underlying idea that feeding too often would cause him to want to eat all the time simply out of habit, even if not hungry.

Imagine the stress of trying to console a hungry baby without feeding him, constantly watching the clock, trying to remember when the last feeding was, all while worrying, "If I don't do this right he'll never sleep through the night! I'll spoil him and create lifelong bad habits for him!" (Which actually translates to, "*I* will never sleep uninterrupted again.") As the final straw, my wonderful husband was not on board with this training, schedule myth and constantly urged me, "Just feed him already!" (easy for him to say with his useless nipples) At the time, that did nothing but add to the stress of the situation, but later I realized how much easier, more peaceful and simple it would have been to follow his uneducated, but wisely instinctual advice and just feed on demand.

Instead of trying to learn how to rigidly implement a strict schedule, why didn't I learn to listen to my baby's cues and physiological design? Why not watch *him* instead of a clock? Why not stop to ask why he might be hungrier at times, or want to cluster feed? Why not ask myself whether *I myself* am always hungry at the exact same time intervals? Could it be that the activities of the day, amount of calories burned, or even growth spurts might affect how often he might be hungry? Could it be that a baby, just like an adult, who hasn't had enough to eat or has felt stressed during the day may not sleep as well during the night?

Asking these kinds of questions would have served me so well! It would have been so much more intuitive to what my baby actually needed while simultaneously taking a huge load off my mind. Because I didn't know better, I was just afraid I'd mess things up and pay for it by forever being nothing but a human pacifier. Think about it though. I was *already* paying a large price with the pressure I was putting on myself and my family by trying to keep a set of rules that weren't working to produce peace. The stressful atmosphere created by trying to get that baby to do what I though he was "supposed to" was a lot worse than if I'd just relaxed, listened to my baby, and allowed myself to be led.

Our first go at potty training was a similar situation. Yes, I've already apologized to my now teenage son for all the guinea pig experiments he got to be part of! I had picked up the idea that kids *had* to be potty trained by the time they were two, and because I was expecting my second baby just after his second birthday, I was even more determined to get the job done before she arrived. Noble aspirations, I know, but once again I was about to find out just how stressful I was capable of making our lives. I'll probably never forget sitting on the bathroom floor with my overly emotional, heavily pregnant self and my precious little toddler, both of us bawling after yet another potty accident. He just wasn't ready and *my* plan was *not* working!

Looking back now, I realize that, both consciously and subconsciously, I thought that in order to be a good mom who's "doing it right", I *had to* do things a very particular way. I didn't properly value individuality or understand that there's no one-size-fits-all, much less that that could be okay. After all, if it worked for my mom, it should work for me, and if it didn't, then I must just not be doing it right! However, that is not what walking in the unforced ryhthms of grace looks like.

Obviously, being led by the Lord rather than by pressure or rules doesn't mean always just going with the flow of whatever requires the least effort. Fighting the good fight of faith, resisting that which is from the enemy, and exercising discipline all require a standing against what would often seem to be the easiest on the flesh. The thing is, doing those things ultimately creates true peace, while only doing what's easiest on the flesh does not. Real, unshakeable peace, as opposed to temporary, fragile, and false peace, should always be the goal.

Heaviness, stress, pressure, and guilt are signs that there's something we're not doing the Lord's way. Jesus said His way is the easy and light way. (Matthew 11:30)

Whether preparing for birth, figuring out parenting, or anything in between, let it all be done in peace, and for peace!

12 healing a broken heart

About a year before we met, a friend of mine had given birth to a stillborn son. One day I began to ask for her perspective on these types of situations that we know are not God's perfect will and plan. She began to respond by saying that the loss of a baby is something you have to be healed *from*. Notice the key word "began". Having ten kids between the two of us at the time, the conversation was unsurprisingly interrupted and we never found our way back to it! However, that one, simple comment stayed with me. More and more, I saw the profound truth of it. When something happens that shouldn't have happened, healing becomes necessary. Grief and brokenness are not something you can hide from, wish away, or just forget over time. You must be *healed*.

If it requires healing, that's evidence it didn't come from God, because things that originate with God don't have to be healed from.

"Does a spring of water bubble out with both fresh water and bitter water? Does a fig tree produce olives, or a grapevine produce figs? No,

185

and you can't draw fresh water from a salty spring." (James 3:11-12 NLT)

Everything produces after its own kind. God is love (I John 4:8), He is good, and does good only (Psalm 119:68). He is incapable of evil, and He is also not confused about what is good and what is evil. Religion teaches that God's definition of good is so different than ours, that it calls evil good. It has conditioned people to believe that God teaches us through pain, loss, sickness, and tragedy, as though He must use and do evil to produce good. "What sorrow for those who say that evil is good and good is evil, that dark is light and light is dark, that bitter is sweet and sweet is bitter." (Isaiah 5:20 NLT) The truth is that the Word of God and the Holy Spirit were given to teach and correct. (John 14:26; John 16:12-15; II Timothy 3:16)

Bad religion told us God would hurt and break us just to prove He could heal us. He would put us through hell just so He could show up as the hero to rescue us.

If a parent were to purposely burn their child's hand over a flame to teach them a lesson, we would call that abusive, sick, and evil. We may even question their mental sanity. Yet, every day, these are the kinds of things people believe about and attribute to God, while simultaneously calling Him "Father". Bluntly put, they believe He is abusive. In presuming that God has to employ evil to accomplish His purposes, they also regard evil as more powerful than good, as if it can produce what the love and goodness of God are powerless to produce.

Friends, if bad things must happen to accomplish God's purposes, then Jesus' death, burial, and resurrection were not enough.

One of the reasons people are so quick to believe that God uses evil to accomplish good is because He is the master at taking what the devil did and meant for evil and turning it around for good. He's that powerful! However, we cannot allow that to confuse us about the sources or fruits of good and evil. Evil didn't *have* to happen in order for good to happen. God didn't *cause* evil *so that* good could come. This is not even possible, because evil cannot produce good, and vice versa. Rather, He caused good to come *in spite of*, and *in the face* of the evil. Evil and darkness are not strong enough to overpower His goodness and love!

I believe the first step to healing of a broken heart, is to settle it in your heart that evil doesn't come from a good God. If you have lost a baby, whether through miscarriage, still birth, or any other way, it wasn't because God needed another flower in His garden or some other ridiculous nonsense, with the assumption that He just has this mysterious plan we are completely incapable of understanding. No, it wasn't because He's trying to teach you a lesson, as if His Word and Spirit are unable to do that job.

"Yea, well, if God is so good, then why did this happen?" God is not intimidated by our questions, but even so, we have to watch that we don't become so desperate to know why that we will believe almost anything just to get a sense of closure or feel like we have an answer. This is a leading reason why so many believe lies about God's nature and character. Attributing the bad thing that happened to the sovereignty of God is the only immediate, so called reason they can come up with that makes any sense to their mind.

As much as we all want to know why, only knowing why doesn't ultimately set you free from grief and pain. Knowing Jesus is what does that. In knowing Jesus, truth is revealed to you. You must keep your focus set on what He shows you and all that you do know, rather than looking at what you don't know. What you don't know is darkness. What you do know is light. How will you find more light by looking for it in the darkness? When you stick with living and walking in the light you have, more light and revelation will come. That is how you get real answers! "In Your light we see light." (Psalm 36:9b NKJV)

One truth you can focus on right now is that God is not the source of tragedy, trauma, or loss. Another truth is that, as a believer, if you've said goodbye to a baby they are with Jesus and you will see them again!

Several years ago, a precious mama from another country shared with me that their baby had been stillborn a few days earlier. What was extraordinary about this story was her response.

"God is good. Satan took something that didn't belong to him, but he's a loser because our baby is safe in Jesus' arms, and I am hidden in Christ, and cannot be snatched from God's hands. I'm sure Satan has long stopped laughing because he no longer has access to harm our son, and he didn't get to even touch my relationship with God. There is not a single doubt in my mind that this was not God's plan for our baby or us. God didn't take our baby, but He has him now. He was a reward from God, and God doesn't reward His children and then take those rewards away. God is good! We have to wait a little bit longer, but we are going to be back, and we are going to take a healthy, living baby home with us."

Just under a year later, they did exactly that!!

Listen to the confidence she had in her source. As a result, healing was already taking place literally within days. Knowing that you know that God is good and not the author of evil is what makes the difference! It doesn't mean there's no pain or that all is easy, but it changes the way you are able to process it. Knowing that He is not the cause of the problem makes it possible to run to Him with complete confidence to be the solution.

On the other hand, as long as you think the unanswered prayers, trauma, loss, and pain have anything to do with His plan or sovereignty, either directly or indirectly by way of permission, there will always be lingering doubts in the back of your mind preventing you from fully trusting Him with your future.

How will you run to Him for answers and help to carry a baby to full term if you believe it was His will for the last pregnancy to end early?

How will you run to Him in faith for healing from grief and trauma if you believe He approved of your pain?

You can't.

"Surely He has borne our griefs and carried our sorrows; yet we esteemed Him stricken, smitten by God, and afflicted. But He was wounded for our transgressions, He was bruised for our iniquities; the chastisement for our peace was upon Him, and by His stripes we are healed." (Isaiah 53:4-5 NKJV)

"The Spirit of the Lord is upon Me, because He has anointed Me to preach the gospel to the poor; He has sent Me to heal the brokenhearted, to proclaim liberty to the captives and recovery of sight to the blind, to set at liberty those who are oppressed; to proclaim the acceptable year of the LORD." (Luke 4:18-19 NKJV)

"He heals the brokenhearted and binds up their wounds." (Psalm 147:3 NKJV) He is the mender of hearts, not the breaker!

Time is not what will heal you. If it could, God would be unnecessary. Likewise, despite the whole world saying you must grieve in order to heal, grieving won't make the pain stop any more than time. Grieving rehearses the pain and trauma, keeping the wounds fresh, and making it impossible to heal. I Thessalonians 4:13 clearly says we shouldn't be overwhelmed with grief like the rest of the world who have no hope, because we don't have to be!

Despite popular thought, it's not true that you will always have to carry grief with you from now on, learning to live with a broken heart that will never fully heal.

Healing takes place when you believe and receive the anointed word God has sent to heal you. (Psalm 107:20) Grief and trauma are under the curse which Jesus, the Word made flesh, came to redeem you from by becoming a curse for you. (Galatians 3:13; John 1:14)

Friends, when Jesus heals, He makes you whole and at peace again, nothing missing and nothing broken. That doesn't mean you have to forget your baby or loved one. You're allowed to wish things were different, and acknowledge that it *should* have been different. It's ok to miss them. Being healed actually sets you free to be able to do that from a place of peace and fondness, rather than feeling like there's a knife in your heart.

To be clear, emotions of sadness, shedding tears, missing someone, or wishing things were different are not automatically tied to a spirit of grief. I'm certainly not advocating for unhealthy suppression of emotions.

The spirit of grief, however, is oppressive and heavy. It makes you feel like you're not really living. It certainly doesn't feel like the abundant life that John 10:10 explicitly tells us Jesus gives. It never lets you rest or come to peace. It won't let you receive God's *healing* comfort. It resists the joy that would be your strength. We are not designed to carry that kind of heavy burden, and it's not God's plan for you.

"To comfort all who mourn, to console those who mourn in Zion, to give them beauty for ashes, the oil of joy for mourning, the garment of praise for the spirit of heaviness; that they may be called trees of righteousness, the planting of the LORD, that He may be glorified." (Isaiah 61:3 NKJV) *That* is God's good plan for you!

Sometimes people are afraid to let go of grief because in their mind, holding on to it keeps them connected in some way to what or who they lost. What they lost was a part of them that has now been replaced with grief, and therefore grief has now become a part of their identity. They're afraid that in letting go of it, they'll again lose a part of themselves. The unwillingness to allow themselves to be healed of grief is rooted in the fear of more pain.

Just as fear is bondage, to live with a spirit of grief is to live in bondage. But where the Spirit of the Lord is, there is freedom! When Jesus, the Truth, makes you free, you are free indeed! (John 8:36)

You can be free from the weight of grief right now! You don't have to wait for a certain amount of time to pass. Pray this prayer: "Jesus, I give you my grief in exchange for your joy and comfort. I thank you for binding up my wounds so they can truly heal. Heal my heart, and set me free to come fully alive once again, living the abundant life You give!"

As you continue to victoriously walk out this journey, make sure the people with whom you have heart-to-heart conversations with are the kind of people with whom you can remain in a spirit of faith and victory. Not everyone will understand why you would even want to resist a spirit of grief. They may conclude that if you can be grateful, happy, positive, and remain standing on God's Word that you are in denial of reality.

Don't give anyone opportunity to drag you down into an atmosphere of grief and suffering.

Now, maybe the hurt you're dealing with is not due to the loss of a child or other loved one, but rather trauma caused by your freedom of choice being taken from you, or other hurtful things done or said to you at your birth.

Maybe it's not birth trauma, but that the baby you're carrying was conceived through a sexual act committed against your will.

Or, maybe the brokenness you need healing for has nothing to do at all with circumstances surrounding conception, pregnancy, or birth, but rather stems from a fragmented relationship you once held dear.

There are numerous different situations in life that can be deeply wounding, but whatever the source of inner pain or brokenness, the answer remains the same. It shouldn't have happened, and therefore, it must be healed from.

If the heart is not healed, no matter the source of pain, the results are still similar. A broken heart that is not healed will usually become a bitter heart. Bitter people are usually such due to the unfair loss of something, whether it be lost dreams, innocence, friendships, marriages, children, opportunities, finances, or anything else.

Hate, unforgiveness, and bitterness always begin with inner pain and offense. The worst part of it is they blind you to truth and light.

"But the one who hates his brother is in the darkness and walks in the darkness, and does not know where he is going because the darkness has blinded his eyes." (I John 2:11 NASB)

If you are in the dark due to unforgiveness and bitterness, how will you see the path you are to take in pregnancy, birth, or life in general? How will you see truth, which is vital to make the best choices? How will you do anything but stumble your way through this journey?

Another thing you become blind to with a broken, unhealed heart is hope, which leads to losing heart.

I was seventeen years old when I entered my first dating relationship. I'd never seen sense in dating someone just for the sake of dating if there was no expectation of a future together. Therefore, I always thought the first and only guy I would date would be the one I'd marry. Now here I was, freshly dumped after a six month relationship I'd thought would lead to marriage. The heartbreak was so intense I immediately became bitter. It felt like my whole world had crashed in on me, making me mad at that entire world. I either ignored or lashed out at those who loved me most. I couldn't see purpose, hope, or joy in anything. The bitterness and unforgiveness had thrown me into the dark, blinding me to truth.

Thank God I could see just enough to know I had to get help. I really wasn't sure I'd make it out alive if something didn't change. Although I wasn't suicidal, it felt like the pain and bitterness would eat at me like a venom from the inside out until I would literally, physically die.

By the grace and mercy of God, and the love and help of my closest friend at the time, I found my way to a pastor I felt I could trust who happened to be in town from across the state. He walked me through the steps of forgiveness and closing the doors I had opened to the enemy, taking back the ground I'd given him. It was as simple as acknowledging the red flags I'd seen and ignored, receiving forgiveness for myself, and then forgiving and releasing my ex from the heart. I crawled into bed in the wee hours of the morning, and when I woke up later that day, I was a totally different person. The weight was gone. The excruciating pain was gone. Suddenly, I could love my family and other people again. I had hope for the future. I could dream again. I could see purpose in life. Once again, the sky was blue, the grass was green, and the sunlight like a kiss from Heaven! I was grateful again!

Make no mistake about it; there were plenty of opportunities to pick the offense and pain back up. Because we were co-workers, I had to face my ex almost every day. I had to choose to forgive many more times. I had to choose to refuse to allow bitterness to creep back in. There were still some painful memories and occurrences, but I was not going back down that dark path. I knew what it was like to be in bondage to bitterness, and I knew what it was like to be free in Christ. Free is better y'all!

Interestingly, only two to three months later I met my real, future husband. What if, at that time, I had still been bitter, blind, and bound? I probably wouldn't even have recognized God's goodness staring me in the face. My guess is that he wouldn't have been attracted to me either, because I was definitely not a pleasant person in that state. Remaining in bondage to a broken heart can alter the entire course of your life.

It's important to note that there's a difference between simply being hurt, and taking offense which results in bitterness. We are human. We will all experience pain at some point. The difference is that people who are simply hurt will look for someone to help them heal, while people who are offended and bitter will look for someone else to hurt.

According to II Corinthians 2:10-11, whether or not you forgive is a determining factor as to whether the devil can exploit, outsmart, or gain advantage over you. Attempting to keep you in unforgiveness is Satan's scheme to legally grant himself continued access to wreak havoc in your life, bringing sickness, loss, and destruction.

Not only that, by using your pain to his advantage, he can extend the damage to others as well. He knows that unforgiving, offended people hurt other people, and so begins a cycle of compounded pain, which often spans multiple generations before someone puts a stop to it. This accomplishes his entire goal.

Forgiveness breaks the enemy's hold on you, cutting off his permission to torment you. It slams the door on him, and opens wide the door to give God access to go to work on your behalf. Forgiveness doesn't right the wrong or make what they did ok, but then again, neither does unforgiveness. What it does do is put the situation in the Lord's hands, Who is the only one who can actually right what needs to be righted, do what man cannot, and work all things together for your good!

Romans 8:28 (NASB), "And we know that God causes all things to work together for good to those who love God, to those who are called according to His purpose." Notice that this promise is for those who love God. I John 4:20 says that if someone claims to love God, yet hates their brother, they are a liar.

Harboring unforgiveness in your heart, which is a degree of hate and the opposite of walking in love, ties the Lord's hands to work things for your good. It's not that He doesn't want to help you or because it's not His will; He simply can't.

The fleshly nature always wants to blame something or someone for our pain. Go ahead and blame the devil! He dreads the day you fully realize he is the only one to blame, because hell has no threat like a mother, father, or anyone else who knows their authority in Christ, knows who their enemy is, and rises up to walk in the victory Jesus already won over him! Satan is already defeated, and when that thief is caught, he must pay!

To experience healing in our lives, whether it be for our bodies, hearts, or minds, we must forgive and walk in love. There's no way around it.

When we are healed, we are free.

When we are free, we are fully alive!

closing

Hey, friend.

Perhaps you've never entered into a personal relationship with God by receiving His gift of grace that erases all your sin, guilt, and condemnation and restores you to intimacy with Him. If that's you, I invite you to pray this prayer.

"Jesus, I believe in my heart that you came as a man to take the punishment for all my wrongdoing and restore me to right standing with God. I believe you died for me and were raised from the dead, destroying the works of the devil and setting me free from all bondage, including fear of any kind. Be the Lord of my life, and lead me into all Your perfect plan for me!" (John 3:16; Romans 5:8-10; Romans 8:1-2; Romans 10:9-10; II Corinthians 5:17-21; I John 2:2)

Perhaps you already know Jesus as your Savior, but as you've read about being individually led by His Spirit, and walking in daily fellowship and intimacy with Him, it has stirred up a desire in you for more. If you have never received the baptism, or infilling, of the Holy Spirit with the evidence of a heavenly prayer language, this prayer is for you.

"Lord Jesus, I ask You according to Your Word in Luke 11:13, to fill me with Your Holy Spirit to overflowing! I receive the promised power to be Your witness!"

Now, by faith, begin to speak out loud the utterance that comes up out of your spirit. It's ok if it seems strange to your natural mind at first. This is not something to be grasped mentally, but with the heart. As you continue to regularly pray in tongues, you will find yourself coming up to a new level of understanding, revelation, and discernment in the things of God and His path for you, developing greater intimacy with Him than you've ever yet known! (Luke 24:49; Acts 1:4-5, 8; Acts 2:4; Acts 8:14-17; Acts 10:44-46; Acts 19:1-6)

Finally, some of you may be struggling to believe that it's not too late for you to fully experience God's goodness, kindness, redemption, and glory.

Perhaps you have found yourself in an unplanned pregnancy as a single mom, and have been told having a baby will change everything, and for the worse. Seeds of doubt have been planted in your mind that you are not strong enough to be a good mother while simultaneously still pursuing your God-given dreams, much less a real relationship with God. You may think your condition has disqualified you and canceled out God's good plan for you. I am telling you, *no, this doesn't change everything!*

Maybe, in some other area of life, you see that you've made poor choices resulting in undesirable circumstances. Maybe you feel that since it's your fault, subsequently, you should have to eat all the bad fruit coming to you, with no hope of being spared that misery.

"But what if some were unfaithful to their divine calling? Does their unbelief weaken God's faithfulness? Absolutely not! God will always be proven faithful and true to His word." (Romans 3:3-4a TPT)

"For the gifts and the calling of God are irrevocable [for He does not withdraw what He has given, nor does He change His mind about those to whom He gives His grace or to whom He sends His call]." (Romans 11:29 AMP)

God's plan for your peace, your welfare, and your bright future has not changed! (Jeremiah 29:11) As you yield to Him, trust Him, and follow Him, He will do far more gloriously good things in and for you than you could ever have asked or imagined. (Ephesians 3:20) He forgives and removes your sins, and because He no longer remembers them, He can bless and prosper you, *no matter what* your past may be. (Hebrews 8:12; Hebrews 10:17; Psalm 103:10-12)

Take heart, beautiful friend, because the Lord loves you as much as He ever has or ever will. Your yes is all it takes to throw wide open the door to all of Him and His goodness. Say yes to Him, His promises, and His Word, and you will live a long, satisfying, abundant life!

notes

1. The work of neuroscientist Dr. Caroline Leaf related to this topic is readily available via her books, podcast, television broadcasts, social media, and more.

2. T.J. Scull et al., "Epidural Analgesia in Early Labour Block the Stress Response but Uterine Contractions Remain Unchanged," Can J Anaesth 45, no.7 (1998): 626-630

R. Jouppila et al., "Maternal and Umbilical Venous Plasma Immunoreactive Beta-Endorphin Levels During Labor With and Without Epidural Analgesia," Am J Obstet Gynecol 147, no. 7 (1983): 799-802

3. Meisenberg an Simmons, 1983

4. C. Thurber, L. R. Dugas, C. Ocobock, B. Carlson, J. R. Speakman, H. Pontzer, "Extreme Events Reveal an Alimentary Limit on Sustained Maximal Human Energy Expenditure." Sci. Adv. 5, eaaw0341 (2019)

5. Jones RK, *Beyond Birth Control: The Overlooked Benefits of Oral Contraceptive Pills*, New York: Guttmacher Institute, 2011

6. Eur Rev Med Pharmacol Sci. 2013 Jul;17(13):1804-13. PMID: 23852908 "Oral Contraceptives and Changes in Nutritional Requirements"

7. Green L, Ottoson J, Garcia C, Hiatt R "Diffusion Theory and Knowledge Dissemination, Utilization, and Integration in Public Health." *Annu Rev Public Health* 2009;30:151-74

Grant J, Green L, Mason B "Basic Research and Health: A Reassessment of the Scientific Basis for the Support of Biomedical Science." *Res Eval* 2003;12:217-24

www.ingramcontent.com/pod-product-compliance
Lightning Source LLC
Chambersburg PA
CBHW070035100426
42740CB00013B/2694